CHRONICALLY IN CHRIST

Smyth & Helwys Publishing, Inc.
6316 Peake Road
Macon, Georgia 31210-3960
1-800-747-3016
©2023 by Julie Owen Morris
All rights reserved.

Library of Congress Cataloging-in-Publication Data on file

Advance Praise for *Chronically in Christ*

Julie's amazing story speaks to those who know the pain, suffering, and struggle of being human as much as to those who deal with chronic illness. Julie acknowledges that there are no easy answers or quick-fix formulas, but there is always hope, and pain can become a friend. The individual devotions become a guide to how one can thrive and not simply survive hardship. For those living in the stress of chaos, Julie's message encourages all of us to remember, "God isn't finished with us yet."

—Dr. Phil Christopher
Consultant, Center for Healthy Churches

Julie writes with wit from a perspective of chronic pain—which may seem to some a bit of a contradiction. Yet in her own words, she neither dismisses her challenges, nor allows the challenges to define her. Julie shares her faith journey as an honest engagement of difficult questions that defy easy answers. Leaning deep into the Scriptures, she emerges with an authentic confession of a life of chronic pain, companioned by the consolations of a faith that does not take away the hardship, but provides a path forward.

—C. Gregory DeLoach, MDiv, DMin
Dean, Mercer University McAfee School of Theology

When yourself or someone you love is in the trenches dealing with a chronic illness you can feel overwhelmed and at times feel hopeless. This book, Chronically In Christ, will renew your hope as read the daily devotions. May you be strengthened day by day with the reminders in these devotions that you are not alone. God is with you on this journey. Yes, the days may be long and some days will be hard, but let God's Truth wash over you as you read the daily devotions and walk beside Julie as she shares her own journey with chronic illness.

—Katrina Dorroh, MDiv
Founder of Faith & Family Box and Popcorn Moments:
Faith & Family Podcast

As one who was first diagnosed with a chronic illness in 2007 and who has lived with that original diagnosis and many others for over fifteen years, Julie Owen Morris sought and found the hope she needed to not only to survive but thrive. Her faith grounded her on her darkest of days, and her faith eventually called her to share this hope with others living with chronic illnesses. She first created a website, then start a devotional blog, and now has written *Chronically in Christ: A Devotional for Those with Chronic Illness*, which includes eighty-one devotions centered on the theme "You are never alone. God is always with you." Morris's words are transparent, vulnerable, and hope filled, never glib, naïve, or blindly optimistic. For those who struggle with the pain and despair of chronic illness, Morris offers an honest and encouraging word of hope.

—*Rev. Dr. Pamela R. Durso*
President, Central Seminary, Shawnee, Kansas

Julie gives glimpses into her "chronically challenged" life that are very different yet eerily similar to my own life. Her shared biblical insights and prayers for her life give me strength and support for living my own life to the fullest.

—*Bo Prosser, EdD*
Catalytic Coach/Consultant
President, Center for Christian Education

Julie Morris is a remarkable follower of Jesus and a very determined human being. As her pastor for a decade, I watched Julie battle her chronic illness with both grit and grace. Her faith, family, and friends empowered her with the resolve and energy to fight her illness daily. Throughout her long struggle, Julie maintained her gentle spirit and joyful demeanor. Readers will be inspired by her insights and story.

—*Dr. R. Mitch Randall*
CEO, Good Faith Media

CHRONICALLY

IN

Christ

A Devotional for Those with Chronic Illness

JULIE OWEN MORRIS

Dedication

To my wonderful family, including my loving husband, Chad; my amazing daughters, Addie and Makenna; my incredible parents, Gayle and Bill; and my entertaining brother, Grant. As the title of the book conveys, I certainly couldn't have made it through all these years of chronic illness without Christ, but I am so thankful that God also gave me all of you to walk alongside me through it all. I can't thank you enough for your love and support.

Also, to all those who suffer daily from chronic illness. I pray that you find an extra dose of hope in these pages through the word of God and the love and strength of Jesus Christ. May you remain chronically in Christ.

Acknowledgments

I must thank, first and foremost, Jesus Christ, who is the source of all my daily strength. I pray that others will find him in these pages. Thank you, Lord, for the great privilege of sharing the pain of my trials with others. I pray that you will turn it all into good by allowing it to encourage others (Rom 8:28).

Thank you to my immediate family, the ones who continually have to put up with my lack of energy, occasional crankiness, and frequent inability to play or go out: Chad, Addie, and Makenna. I love you each more than you will ever understand. Thank you to my first family: my beyond-wonderful Mom and Dad—Gayle and Bill—and my ornery but funny brother Grant. Thank you also to my incredible in-laws, Linda and Troy, and my sisters-in-law, Shell and Lisa, for sharing Chad with me. My extended family has also been very supportive, particularly my Aunt Gayla, Uncle Chuck, and cousin/friend Brandi.

My lifelong childhood friends have walked with me through junior high, high school, college life, children's births, divorce, single motherhood, and decades of chronic illness, and they all deserve a medal: Sheri, Monica, Alicia, Katrina, Rhonda, Stephanie, and Jaronica. My newer later-in-life friends Cheryl, Angela, Stephanie, Tonya, Chevas, Kim, Divina, and Gala have each added such delight to my life. Gala has stretched my thinking and increased my faith through all her challenging book and Bible studies, and she has been persistent in encouraging my writing. Thank you to Brenda, who took me to my first lupus support group and who walks the lupus path with me. Thank you *all*—I have the best friends on earth!

Thank you to Keith, Leslie, and the whole team at Smyth & Helwys for giving me the opportunity to encourage others through this book. Thank you, Stephanie (yes—I have three friends named

Stephanie!), for your generous and wise marketing advice to help get this book into the hands of those who need a little hope.

Thank you to my many, many doctors but particularly Dr. Carson, Dr. LePine, and Dr. Ghezzi for your continual compassion and persistence in working to solve the issues of autoimmune disease. I wish everyone had great doctors like you!

Finally, thank you, readers, for taking the time to reach for hope in God's word. I pray that this book encourages you and that you will never give up until you find healing spiritually, emotionally, and physically. I love you and I care.

This is why we work hard and continue to struggle, for our hope is in the living God, who is the Savior of all people and particularly of all believers.

—1 Timothy 4:10 (NLT)

Contents

Introduction

Like many others, I didn't discover my chronic illness when my life was calm, peaceful, and happy. Instead, it crashed right into the midst of chaos. As an example, here's how the year 2007 began for me:

January 2007: "Your house is on fire. Get your child out now."
February 2007: "I'm sorry, but we can't ignore these symptoms any longer. I must formally diagnose you with systemic lupus erythematosus (SLE)."
March 2007: "I woke up this morning and everything's different. I don't love you the same, and I want a divorce."

Yes, it was quite a start to a new year, facing a lupus diagnosis while displaced from my home due to a house fire. Add to that a husband who had been gone all hours of the night for months and then suddenly decided he wanted a divorce.

The focus of this book is chronic illness, which, as I know too well, often occurs in the middle of a life already full of stress. Stress is not the only factor, as most chronic illnesses are multifactorial, but stress can definitely push us over the edge into a lifelong illness. The house would eventually get fixed although I could not afford it at the time since I was going through a divorce. The divorce took care of the bad marriage, but it would be years until I found stable ground and could see it as a blessing.

The lupus, however, could not be fixed. Ever. I realized that I was stuck with it for the rest of my life. At first, I thought that meant imminent death, thanks to a quick trip around Google. After my panic subsided, I realized that I had to get and stay healthy enough to be a single mother to my (then) three-year-old daughter. My divorce lawyer told me that if I became disabled, I would lose custody of her. Sure, that was very helpful for my stress level.

So how did I make it? I'll admit that at times it seemed impossible and overwhelming. I survived through God's love and comfort, the best parents and family, truly wonderful friends, a supportive church, and the sweet, comforting laughter of my daughter. Daily time with God, prayer, and Bible reading were the keys to sanity for me.

Fast-forward six years, and here's what I wrote in my journal in 2013:

> Where did time go? Well, I've been busy! So busy that I strengthened my faith (or, rather, allowed God to strengthen my faith), found a combination of medications to help my lupus, met a man, fell in love (REALLY this time!), married that man, had another beautiful baby daughter, moved, and tried a new direction in my career. I TOLD you I had been busy! My husband always jokes that we met in May of 2010, married in May of 2011, and had our baby in May of 2012. He wanted to know what we were planning for May of 2013. NOTHING! We rested and then celebrated Chuck E. Cheese style, with a combined birthday party for our two girls: one turning nine and the other turning one. I must say, life is good. No, I mean really good. Truly. Peacefully, low stress, comfortable, lovely good. Marriage (this time) is what I think God intends it to be. Motherhood is exhausting but joy-filled. Work is fun. Faith is fulfilling.

Some of you might be thinking something like, "Good for you, Julie. You got your life together. You have peace. Your chronic illness is better. What about me? Life is *not* good for me; life is full of stress and fear." To you, I say I am so sorry. There are no easy answers. Do I understand your life? No. Have I lived the choking, gasping, minutes of your life when you are straining to take that next step, struggling for a sip of air? No. I do not know what your life is. I do not know how you deal with the things you face.

All I can know is my own struggles, my four single-mom years of disease-ridden struggle, when my close friend Sheri kept saying it was going to get better and I looked at her with my hollow eyes, pale skin, and skinny, ill body and explained to her how it was even worse each week. I told her to stop her weekly pep talks because they just weren't true. But that stubborn woman wouldn't listen. That stubborn, strong, faith-filled woman kept trying to encourage me when it was aggravating and I wanted her to give up. I wanted her to admit that my life was *bad*, that it was even worse than it was a month ago, and that there was no reason to hope. She wouldn't. And you know what? Sheri was right! Things *did* get better, but that didn't happen after a year or even two years. It took a few years, and it was a gradual healing. It didn't happen the way I prayed it would. Still, in God's timing, something good happened. Now my life is better than it ever was before 2007.

Will this happen for you? Can your life turn around? Could you actually begin to have less stressful, less painful, and more joyful days? Can your chronic illness improve?

I sure hope so. In fact, I pray so! I am praying for you, my readers, as I write this. I pray for hope and joy and healing through Christ.

What I have learned about chronic illness over the years is that it is unpredictable. I've had days when I can't move and can't get out of bed, when I feel so bad that I can't even read or watch TV. I've also had days when I almost felt like a normal person (although I'm not sure I have a good grasp of normal after eighteen years of chronic illness). I tend to collect diagnoses the same way I do china teacups. I have lupus (SLE, my worst chronic illness); psoriatic arthritis; psoriasis; Sjogren's syndrome; Hashimoto's thyroiditis; fibromyalgia; ulcerative colitis; migraines; mitral valve prolapse syndrome; peripheral neuropathy; Raynaud's syndrome; interstitial cystitis; intestinal permeability; scoliosis with chronic back pain; dysbiosis; POTS; and food sensitivities. I'm sure I'm forgetting some, but you get the picture. Every time I go to a new doctor, they say something like, "Wow—you've got a lot going on here," which translates to "You are a medical mess."

So now I'm going to tell you how to turn your life around and get better in five easy steps.

No, I'm not. I wish I could, but there's no easy formula. And I don't know how to help you turn *your* life around. I don't know how

4 CHRONICALLY IN CHRIST

to help you in your illness. However, I think I may be able to help you, at least a little, learn to get through it daily. If you can dream with me, though, I want even more than that for you.

My rheumatologist has a fundraising T-shirt printed each year. My favorite one reads, "I'm not trying to just survive, but to thrive!" That is what I want for you: not just to survive your chronic illness (or illnesses) with God's help, but to thrive through it all.

I can tell you how God worked in my life and about the Scriptures and people God has utilized to help me cope as I not so patiently waited for the big 180. As I gradually found the hope I needed through Christ to live with daily chronic illness and all the pain and sickness it entails, I began to want to share this hope with others who were suffering.

I kept getting a nudge during church and during prayer to start a website with a devotional blog for people with chronic illness. I didn't *want* to, as I'm an introvert and I didn't know anything about such technology. But that nudge, those thoughts, simply wouldn't fade.

Around the same time, I was going to monthly infusion labs (which I did for over four years) to receive chemo for lupus. During this time, I saw sick people, sicker than I was, whose eyes looked hollow and hopeless. I tried to talk with them without intruding on their privacy. I often thought, "How do people handle this without Jesus?" I couldn't get this question out of my mind.

After a year of resisting that nudge from God, I started a website: chronicallyinchrist.com. A year later, I linked it to a devotional blog. I began writing a blog post once a week, except when I was too sick to manage it. I learned how to link it to Pinterest to reach a bigger audience. Then I felt that it was time for the next step. I decided to put my devotions in a book in order to reach a new group of people who suffer with chronic illness. You are now reading that book.

My sincere prayer is to give you hope in Christ. I want to help you through your illness, whatever it is. I want you to thrive with Christ, to know that you're not done on this earth. You have kingdom work to do. You may wonder about those days when you're too sick to work. You can still pray, and I firmly believe that prayer is powerful work.

I hope that I can be a source of strength for you through this book. I hope my words help you realize that you are not the only one facing life with a chronic illness. Most of all, I pray that this book helps you find the hope you need to try again another day. The key is Jesus Christ. May the God of peace provide you with hope and strength through him.

The last thing a person with chronic illness needs to feel, once again, that they let down themselves or others with something they just don't feel well enough to do. With that in mind, this is not a daily or weekly devotional, but an anytime devotional. Reach for this book whenever you are able and when you need a little encouragement to continue the fight with hope.

I would also like to offer you the prayers of a fellow sufferer. If you would like me to pray for you specifically, I would be honored. Please write to me at hope@chronicallyinchrist.com.

1. A Firm Foundation (even when it seems like a Jell-O walk)

The fundamental fact of existence is that this trust in God, this faith, is the firm foundation under everything that makes life worth living. —Hebrews 11:1 (NLT)

Being a Christian does not solve our problems. It does not protect us from devastation or tragedy. Being a Christian does not isolate us from people who will hurt us. It does not keep us from getting really sick.

Where did people get the idea that they should not have trouble because they are "good"? In the Bible, Jesus says that in this world we will face many trials and sorrows, but we should take heart because God has overcome the world (John 16:33). The world—with all its problems, with our sorrow, with our loved one's betrayal, or with our chronic illness—will not have the last word. God will. We have the assurance that God is in control and will work it all out in the end.

Faith can give us this comforting assurance that someday (maybe in this life or maybe later) God will fix everything. Once we give in to the fact that it probably won't be tomorrow or next week, we can rest and live in this truth each day. How? Faith gives us strength to go on and strength for each day, each hour, each minute. Faith is the "firm foundation" under everything that makes life worth living!

If you are a Christian, if you have faith in God, if you trust in and seek God, you can have strength enough for each day. If you are in a difficult situation, a fearful situation, or excruciating pain, you can still take the next step and live the next day because you are walking in faith. If you are in pain or so sick that you can't leave your bed, you can cry out to God to help you through the next moment.

During my worst times back in 2007, I would survive a week of work, a sick child, arthritis pain and fever/fatigue, bill collectors calling, and a court date, and then I would look back and wonder how I got through it all. The answer was always God—strength from my faith. How do people who do not have faith survive a divorce or a house fire or a chronic illness (or all three at once)? I truly have no idea.

Were there weeks when I felt like I might crumble? Times when I could not feel the strength of my faith? Of course! My faith was there, but I couldn't grasp it. That's when I needed the support of others. My family, my church family, and my Christian friends were a huge source of strength for me. Their firm foundation seemed more obvious than mine at that moment, so I borrowed energy from one or two of them.

If you don't have anyone to lean on (or could use a little extra encouragement), then lean on me through this book. You are not alone in your chronic illness, and I promise you that there is reason to hope.

Lord, when everything feels shaky and insecure, help us to feel your firm foundation. Please nudge these fellow sufferers toward your strength and hope, through Jesus Christ. Help them to never, ever give up. Amen.

2. Hope? Yes . . . Mostly

Instead, you must worship Christ as Lord of your life. And if someone asks about your hope as a believer, always be ready to explain it. —1 Peter 3:15 (NLT)

It's easy to fall into depression and sadness when you're in pain. Yesterday, after a night with a migraine, I woke up in the morning with terrible back and neck pain. I didn't want to move. At first, I thought I *couldn't* move. Those of you with arthritis know what I'm talking about—that initial paralyzing stiffness and pain that makes getting up and brushing your teeth seem completely impossible. My body told me to give up, but my mind and soul disagreed. I eventually began to stretch out and limp to the bathroom.

What makes me keep getting up each morning even when I'm in significant pain? Jesus. I have hope because I know Jesus. I know that I can get up, grab some coffee and my Bible, and stumble outside to spend time with him. After a few minutes of praying, Bible reading, and looking at nature, I am eventually glad that I got up. I am actually thankful that I get another day on this earth.

I feel Jesus's presence and know that I am never alone in my pain; Jesus Christ is always with me. The good thing is that talking to Jesus takes little energy and effort. When I do, I feel connected to him. He's always ready to listen, even if all I can manage is a cry of help through the pain.

Jesus, please be with those who face a pattern of pain and illness. Provide comfort with your presence each day. Amen.

3. Pushed Past Your Limit

No test or temptation that comes your way is beyond the course of what others have had to face. All you need to remember is that God will never let you down, he'll never let you be pushed past your limit; he'll always be there to help you come through it. —1 Corinthians 10:13 (MSG)

Have you ever felt pushed past your limit? This can be an emotional/psychological limit or a physical pain limit. Going through my divorce (and then unwanted separation from my child for visitation) seemed beyond what I could take. Last year, I had an ovarian torsion; that pain was unimaginable. I've had many migraines that were unbearable. Sometimes just the consistency and lack of relief from pain (like daily arthritis) can seem impossible to handle.

However, I somehow made it through the above situations that seemed to push me past my limit at the time. How? It was not my strength but God's strength. My strength was gone, but God was there to help me through. Honestly, it often felt like God dragged me through it. I was exhausted coming out the other side, but I wasn't alone.

Look at 1 Corinthians 10:13 again. See those absolutes: "never," "never," and "always." Those are strong words that give me hope. If you feel stretched past your limit today, rest in those promises. You are *never alone*. God is *always* with you.

Dear God, thank you for the promise that you are always with me and you will always help me through the impossible pain. Help me to remember this when I am hurting so deeply. Amen.

4. Use Your Brain

God wants us to use our intelligence, to seek to understand as well as we can. —1 Corinthians 12:2 (MSG)

When we read 1 Corinthians 12:2 within the context of the verses around it, I think Paul is saying to use our intelligence to think about and discern what is right and which path we should take. We shouldn't blindly follow others but instead think through our choices and do the right thing.

In addition to morality and ethics, however, I believe this verse can apply to many other areas of our lives. In terms of illness, I think we should try to be informed. Research your disease or diagnosis; research all treatments (including medications and supplements and alternative treatments and nutrition). Think through all the information and decide what is right for you. Why should you blindly follow one doctor's advice? By educating yourself, you empower yourself, and you can work together with your providers to find the best combinations of treatments and lifestyle changes.

As an example, over the past year I researched an off-label use for a medication, brought the research to my rheumatologist, and started a new treatment that has helped. Then I sought the advice of a functional medicine doctor and dietician, and my gastrointestinal symptoms have drastically improved in a way they hadn't before, when I was only following the advice of my conventional gastroenterologist. Be your own advocate and researcher. Fight for yourself! Use your brain. If you don't know where to begin, I have a page of resources on my website: chronicallyinchrist.com/resources. I sincerely hope that you find something that helps you in your own research.

Dear Lord, help me to use the intelligence you've given me to live the life you intended for me. Please lead me to the right resources and point me in the right direction. Amen.

5. Hope Unswervingly

But for right now, until that completeness, we have three things to do to lead us toward that consummation: Trust steadily in God, hope unswervingly, love extravagantly. And the best of the three is love. —1 Corinthians 13:13 (MSG)

Let me tell you (perhaps a little late) why I wrote this book. I've been living with lupus and other autoimmune diseases for eighteen years. There's no downplaying it; my life is *hard*. The main key for people like you and me is hope. When the pain is severe, we've got to hope that we will be better in an hour or in a day. We've got to hope that a better treatment or a cure will someday make life less difficult. I find my daily hope in Jesus.

After over four years in the infusion lab (every four weeks), I kept hurting for the others I saw there. The mood was mostly depressive and sad. Everyone there was very sick, but I wanted so much to help the ones who were obviously suffering, the ones who seemed to have the light draining from their eyes. I felt that they needed a reason to hope. As I mentioned, I believe the main, sustaining daily source of hope is found in Jesus Christ. I began to wonder how people can make it through daily suffering without him. My prayer is that through this devotional, I may lead someone to find the sustaining, life-giving hope of Christ.

In addition, in all the years that I have been sick, I have learned a few things: where to find trusted resources, some products that have helped, and the value of real, organic food (mostly vegetables). I wish I had known these things in the first few years of my diseases. Perhaps I could have slowed the progression of symptoms. By sharing some of these things, I pray that someone with chronic illness will find something that may improve a symptom or two. Everyone is different, but we're all searching for relief.

Do I always hope *unswervingly*? No, definitely not, but I have some level of hope each day. That's what keeps me fighting and moving forward. That constant, unswerving kind of hope is a goal of mine. I've found that spending time with Jesus gets me closer.

Dear God, help me to connect with you. Thank you for the gift of hope. Thank you that you never give up on me and I'm never alone in my pain. Please help my hope to become more constant. Amen.

6. Lack of Energy

It was God giving me the work to do, God giving me the energy to do it. —1 Corinthians 15:11 (MSG)

Do you ever wake up in the morning and think, "No—I can't do today. I have zero energy"? Many people with an autoimmune disease often feel that they don't have enough energy to get up and brush their teeth, much less do substantial work. I've been there repeatedly.

If this is you today, try not to stress about it. Zero in on the one most important thing to get done, and ask God for the energy to accomplish it. Maybe it's fixing breakfast for your kids. Maybe it's watering your plants or feeding the cat. Maybe it's sending an encouraging text to a friend who is struggling. Usually you can accomplish one thing, however small.

People with chronic illness often have to make huge adjustments to their expectations of themselves. Their bodies can't keep up with what they wish to accomplish. It's extremely frustrating, but it gets a bit easier with time. Sometimes they have to change career paths or stop working outside the home. It's difficult to admit that we can't rely on our bodies for what we need them to do.

Personally, I had to stop seeing patients, and I now work part-time from home. I did not want to quit, and I still miss my work, but my body (or diseases) wouldn't allow me to continue. So I had to adjust. I had to give myself some grace, recognize that there is value in what I can still do, and ask God daily for enough energy to do it.

Dear God, please give me just enough energy for today. Help me to do your work and help me to go a little easier on myself when I fall short. Amen.

7. Alongside You

All praise to the God and Father of our Master, Jesus the Messiah! Father of all mercy! God of all healing counsel! He comes alongside us when we go through hard times, and before you know it, he brings us alongside someone else who is going through hard times so that we can be there for that person just as God was there for us. We have plenty of hard times that come from following the Messiah, but no more so than the good times of his healing comfort—we get a full measure of that, too. —2 Corinthians 1:3-5 (MSG)

Like so many others with chronic illness, as I write this I've been stuck at home for three and a half months now. Hiding from Covid-19 is getting old, but I'm told that's what I must do. The risk is too high, and I need to be here for my children. However, so much time at home makes life feel small and limited.

In this time of isolation, I struggle with the "works" part of my faith. Other than taking care of my immediate family, what am I supposed to be doing? How can I reach others, encourage others, and share Christ when I see no one?

These devotions and my accompanying website are part of my solution. In the verses above, I read that God has been beside me throughout my diseases, complications, and now isolation. I want to come alongside you. I want to help you in any small way possible. I want to help you not simply endure but also find joy and hope amid pain and isolation. It's really possible. Verse 5 talks about the Messiah's "healing comfort." That's what I feel, and I really want you to experience it as well. After all, isn't healing comfort what we're all seeking?

Lord of healing comfort, touch the lives of those who are suffering daily. Help them to feel your presence. Please provide them with enough hope and strength for this day. Amen.

8. Tired of this Body

For instance, we know that when these bodies of ours are taken down like tents and folded away, they will be replaced by resurrection bodies in heaven—God-made, not hand-made—and we'll never have to relocate our "tents" again. Sometimes we can hardly wait to move—and so we cry out in frustration. Compared to what's coming, living conditions around here seem like a stopover in an unfurnished shack, and we're tired of it! We've been given a glimpse of the real thing, our true home, our resurrection bodies! The Spirit of God whets our appetite by giving us a taste of what's ahead. He puts a little of heaven in our hearts so that we'll never settle for less. —2 Corinthians 5:1-5 (MSG)

I had two migraine days this week, and I'm sick of them. When I have a migraine, I can't function well. Not only was my head pounding with pain, but I couldn't think straight and felt like throwing up. Migraines (or any other kind of acute sickness) always further aggravate my arthritis so that I hurt everywhere—not just my head.

When I feel like that, it's easy to get discouraged. I start thinking that life is terrible and I will always feel terrible. I start thinking that I'm a bad mother, as my younger daughter was watching too much TV since I was lying in a dark room, unable to interact with her. I start thinking that life is always going to be this way.

I have to remind myself that it's temporary. As the passage from 2 Corinthians 5 tells me, those terrible living conditions do not last forever. Thankfully, I didn't have to wait until I was in my "resurrection body" to get some relief. I'm much better today. I can think and do chores and interact with my family. For that, I'm very grateful.

I'm also grateful for the reminder that I won't struggle with chronic illness forever.

Dear Lord, help us through pain and sickness. We get so frustrated and tired sometimes. Remind us that it won't last forever, but also please give us some relief now. Help us feel your very real presence, even in our pain. Amen.

9. Power Tools

The world is unprincipled. It's dog-eat-dog out there! The world doesn't fight fair. But we don't live or fight our battles that way—never have and never will. The tools of our trade aren't for marketing or manipulation, but they are for demolishing that entire massively corrupt culture. We use our powerful God-tools for smashing warped philosophies, tearing down barriers erected against the truth of God, fitting every loose thought and emotion and impulse into the structure of life shaped by Christ. Our tools are ready at hand for clearing the ground of every obstruction and building lives of obedience into maturity. —2 Corinthians 10:3-6 (MSG)

Some days I feel like the world is crashing. Can anyone else relate? As I write this, Covid-19 is everywhere, seemingly out of control. I haven't been to a restaurant, church, or mall in four months—that's major social isolation. Isolation is common for those of us with poor immune systems, who had to be extremely cautious in public places during cold and flu season, even before Covid. The battle for racial equality continues in a frustratingly slow manner. Lying is so accepted these days in news and politics that I can't find the truth, even though I'm diligently seeking it.

Have you ever heard the song "Surrounded" by Michael W. Smith? It talks about God surrounding us when we are fighting battles. When I need to know that I'm not alone and the world is not crashing, I listen to this song. It reminds me that God is in control and stands with me, all around me.

All I have to do is remind myself that God is there and that I can seek God. I can draw strength from God. When I do, my "power tools" are ready. I am not helpless after all.

Thank you, God, for surrounding us in the midst of chaos. Thank you for providing your "powerful God-tools" for us. Help us use them carefully to build lives of obedience to you. Amen.

10. Strength in Weakness

Because of the extravagance of those revelations, and so I wouldn't get a big head, I was given the gift of a handicap to keep me in constant touch with my limitations. Satan's angel did his best to get me down; what he in fact did was push me to my knees. No danger then of walking around high and mighty! At first, I didn't think of it as a gift, and begged God to remove it. Three times I did that, and then he told me,

My grace is enough; it's all you need.
My strength comes into its own in your weakness.

Once I heard that, I was glad to let it happen. I quit focusing on the handicap and began appreciating the gift. It was a case of Christ's strength moving in on my weakness. Now I take limitations in stride, and with good cheer, these limitations that cut me down to size—abuse, accidents, opposition, bad breaks. I just let Christ take over! And so, the weaker I get, the stronger I become. —2 Corinthians 12:7-10 (MSG)

I've spent a lot of time thinking about this passage over the years, particularly how it relates to my chronic illness. How many times have I begged God to remove my multiple diseases? It's a good day for me when I can find some benefit to my weakness and sickness. The benefit is that it requires me to lean on God more and on myself less.

How does this work? I know I don't have the strength many days to get through what I need to do. However, this passage reminds me that God definitely has the strength. The next step is to pray for strength. I rely on God. That's the only way for me to get through the day.

Simply realizing that my weakness requires me to depend more on God's strength benefits me in the short term, but it has also made a huge difference over the years. The more I make a habit of relying on God's strength rather than my own, the better life is and the closer I feel to Jesus. This type of submission takes discipline and practice, but it's worth it.

If you're having a day that feels impossible, just admit that you are too weak for this. Pray to God and rely on God's strength to get you through. God will never abandon you.

Lord God, thank you that your strength takes over in my weakness. Help me to reach out and rely on you. Remind me that I don't need to suffer through this alone. Amen.

11. Good Distress?

Distress that drives us to God does that. It turns us around. It gets us back in the way of salvation. We never regret that kind of pain. But those who let distress drive them away from God are full of regrets, end up on a deathbed of regrets.
—2 Corinthians 7:10 (MSG)

The *New Oxford American Dictionary* defines distress as "extreme anxiety, sorrow, or pain." Isn't it the perfect time for distress? There are all kinds of distress in our world right now. There is distress from fear and anxiety over acute disease, such as Covid, flu, pneumonia, and from surgeries and hospital stays. Sometimes my prayer list for those I know are physically suffering is so long that I get overwhelmed. We can't help but worry about our loved ones who are sick. We worry about our loved ones and ourselves. We want to know when it will all end, but there are no answers. Those who have the virus, as well as their families, are enduring extreme pain and suffering. There is sorrow for so many families whose loved ones have lost the fight.

In addition to this, there's plenty of many other sources of pain and tragedy. I know someone who just lost her husband to a car wreck. I recently had a relative die of a stroke. Many people suffer daily debilitating pain from chronic conditions like psoriatic arthritis and multiple sclerosis. Countless people have lost their jobs and wonder how they will feed their children. People continue to face abuse, neglect, betrayal, and injustice every day.

All of this can be extremely overwhelming. How do we choose to respond? Second Corinthians 7:10 says that when distress drives us to God, it turns us around. I think most of us could use a turn-around, a life change, a refocus on what is truly important. Whether you're facing coronavirus in your family or daily back pain, try your best to turn toward God rather than away. Spend time in prayer and deep thought over the direction of your life. This time of pain just might bring forth something fruitful for you.

Dear Lord, we are very distressed. Help us to turn towards you in our pain. Please offer us a glimmer of hope for the future. Sustain us and strengthen us and help us to feel your presence. Amen.

12. God Wants Me Strong?

And that about wraps it up. God is strong, and he wants you strong. So, take everything the Master has set out for you, well-made weapons of the best materials. And put them to use so you will be able to stand up to everything the Devil throws your way. This is no afternoon athletic contest that we'll walk away from and forget about in a couple of hours. This is for keeps, a life-or-death fight to the finish against the Devil and all his angels. —Ephesians 6:10-12 (MSG)

Do you feel strong today? I don't. I did a chore and now I'm completely wiped out. This is typical of me—as a person with lupus, I am constantly tired and weak. Strong is not a word I use to describe myself. As mentioned before in this book, the Bible teaches us that Christ's strength works through our own weakness (see 2 Corinthians 12). I find comfort in that.

I also believe, however, that the above passage from Ephesians tells us that God gives us tools to make us stronger. While I think today's passage is mainly focused on spiritual tools (which I can gain by connecting myself to Christ), it also makes me think about other types of tools God gives me to increase my strength. I think we can all agree that there are various kinds of strength: spiritual, emotional, physical. For emotional strength, I know that God has provided me with family and friends. For physical strength, God has provided me with knowledge about good, organic food and supplements, the right kinds of gentle exercise, and more.

Do I take full advantage of these tools every day? Do I spend time with God? Do I connect with people? Do I choose to reach for celery or potato chips? Do I utilize all the tools I have to gain strength?

Dear Lord, thank you for the tools for strength that you have provided. Help me to make wise choices and help me to grow in strength in all ways. Amen.

13. Beautiful and Whole

But there's far more to life for us. We're citizens of high heaven! We're waiting the arrival of the Savior, the Master, Jesus Christ, who will transform our earthy bodies into glorious bodies like his own. He'll make us beautiful and whole with the same powerful skill by which he is putting everything as it should be, under and around him. —Philippians 3:20-21 (MSG)

Are you craving a body transformation? Do you need one? I haven't felt that my body was beautiful and whole since my twenties. I'm not speaking of aging here but of disease. My body is broken. With lupus and psoriasis come all kinds of rashes and dark spots and sores. What's worse, though, is the joint pain and the migraines and the fever and the nausea. You get the picture. It's not a wholesome, beautiful picture.

I don't write every week because I can't. I have some days/weeks when I can't manage anything. Last week, one of those days was Tuesday, when I woke up with more stiffness and joint pain than usual. I hobbled around to feed the dog and my daughter, and then a migraine set in that didn't go away until the next day. This migraine was paralyzing; I couldn't read or look at a screen or move. I hurt everywhere. I had to lie in a dark room with an eye mask for hours and hours. I couldn't even think straight.

When I have those kinds of days, the only prayers I can utter are "help" and "be with me" and "make it stop." That's okay. I firmly believe God was with me the whole time and helped me through the suffering, minute by minute. God can help you, too, in your throbbing-pain minutes.

The next morning, I awoke with only a hint of the headache left. I was so relieved. Then I read the above passage from Philippians, reminding me that it wouldn't always be like this, that one day I will be transformed and be "beautiful and whole." Everything (my body *and* the world) will one day be as it should be. I need to know and believe this. Don't you?

Dear Lord, help us through the throbbing, pain-filled moments of life. We long for relief. Keep reminding us that it won't always be like this. Thank you for your promises. Amen.

14. What Are You Thinking On?

Summing it all up, friends, I'd say you'll do best by filling your minds and meditating on things true, noble, reputable, authentic, compelling, gracious—the best, not the worst; the beautiful, not the ugly; things to praise, not things to curse. Put into practice what you learned from me, what you heard and saw and realized. Do that, and God, who makes every-thing work together, will work you into his most excellent harmonies. —Philippians 4:8-9 (MSG)

I read a headline yesterday and immediately felt my chest tighten. While I'm usually not that in tune with my body (although I should be), I immediately knew that my body was reacting negatively and I needed to take a break. Then last night, my mom said she had seen something on Facebook that disturbed her so much that she had to take medicine to relax. It got me thinking about what we're all thinking about these days.

While I believe we need to be generally informed about local, state, national, and global events, do we need to seek out and dwell on every detail? Is too much bad news bad for our health? I don't know about you, but this topic has come up for me many times during the Covid-19 pandemic. I stay informed, but I've learned to limit my exposure. How much time do you really need to spend on political news, violence, war footage, etc.? You have to find your own balance. For me, that's a limit of fifteen to thirty minutes of news per day (including reading and watching). Of course, you can also extend this warning to the movies you watch, the music you listen to, the books you read, etc.

Pay attention to your body: is there any tightness, muscle strain, shallow breathing? If you're stressed or anxious, give both your body and mind a break—fill yourself with true, noble, beautiful, praise-worthy thoughts. I do this by reading the Bible or an uplifting book or listening to an inspiring song. Sometimes I just need a light, calm novel to relax my brain so that I can rest. Your body is already stressed with illness, so please don't add to the stress unnecessarily.

Dear Lord, thank you for advising us on what is best for our minds and our health. In an information-driven world, give us the discipline to limit ourselves for better emotional, spiritual, and physical health. Help us to take better care of ourselves. Amen.

15. Meaningful Work

Be assured that from the first day we heard of you, we haven't stopped praying for you, asking God to give you wise minds and spirits attuned to his will, and so acquire a thorough understanding of the ways in which God works. We pray that you'll live well for the Master, making him proud of you as you work hard in his orchard. As you learn more and more how God works, you will learn how to do your work. We pray that you'll have the strength to stick it out over the long haul—not the grim strength of gritting your teeth but the glory-strength God gives. It is strength that endures the unendurable and spills over into joy, thanking the Father who makes us strong enough to take part in every-thing bright and beautiful that he has for us. —Colossians 1:9-12 (MSG)

As my lupus progressed, I started catching everything. After I endured infection after infection and took daily antibiotics without success, my doctor gently suggested that it was time to consider quitting my job. The daily contact with patients was exposing me to too many bacteria and viruses. Eventually, I realized he was right, but what would I do? I had decided to be an SLP (speech-language patholo-gist) when I was seventeen and never looked back. I loved my work and hated to give it up. I felt lost, but then God reminded me that I had always wondered what teaching would be like. God provided a part-time teaching job at two different universities for five years. When that became too exhausting for me, God provided a part-time online teaching job. This was the perfect fit, as I could work from my couch or bed. On really bad days or days when I had infusions, I could skip most of my work, choosing to put off grading papers until the next day.

I still teach college classes online as an adjunct professor. Is it my dream job? Absolutely not, but it is a job, and I've come to realize that it is truly meaningful work. In addition to indirectly helping children (as I teach these students to work with children), I am also helping the students to better their lives with a good career. It's not what I set out to do, but it's still kingdom work.

There are countless types of meaningful work. Putting in a load of laundry is taking care of your family (as I reminded myself this morning when I did it). Volunteering or giving money to a food bank are both meaningful. Maybe you are bed-bound today, feeling useless, and thinking there's nothing meaningful that you can contribute. I've been there, but there may be things you can still do. You can text an encouraging word to a friend. You can write down your health struggles and maybe choose to share them with someone else who suffers. You can read a book to a child; sometimes that's the only sort of interaction I can manage with my child on a bad day.

If you are so sick today that you can do absolutely nothing, you can still pray and call out to God for help. Please remember that you are never alone. You can be with God, and that is always meaningful.

Dear Lord, we crave meaningful work in our lives. We want our lives to matter—to you and to others. Please strengthen us so that we can complete the work that you've given us today. Help us to feel your presence. Amen.

16. Green Hope

May the God of green hope fill you up with joy, fill you up with peace, so that your believing lives, filled with the life-giving energy of the Holy Spirit, will brim over with hope!
—Romans 15:13 (MSG)

Writing this book is my feeble attempt to give you hope—hope to make it through the sick days and the painful minutes that tick by so slowly. I want you to hope for a better tomorrow. Hope for a cure. Hope for healing.

I firmly believe God loves to give us hope, but we get so worn down and stuck in the monotony of our illnesses that we often can't summon even a glimmer of hope. This week, I found some "green hope."

Since a normal vacation is out of the question for an immuno-compromised person during the first year of Covid-19, we had to get creative. Five months isolated at home can really get to a person! A couple of times during the summer of 2020, my family rented a house nearby. We went in with masks, gloves, Clorox, and Lysol and thoroughly cleaned first thing. Then we settled in and relaxed.

The location one week was a pool-house cottage on a ranch. Sitting by the pool (with a waterfall and a hot tub!) one evening, pondering the Bible and talking to God, I watched the horses and cows graze on the green grass. There, I found some hope. It was peaceful and relaxing, and something about gazing at the grass and flowers and trees was rejuvenating. It was good for my soul. It gave me hope—for my illness, for the pandemic to eventually end, and for a better future.

I pray that you can find some green hope this week. Could you drive to a lake and listen to the lapping water? Could you sit on your back porch and gaze at the squirrels playing in the trees? Could you walk or drive to a local park? Could you relax in a hammock? Seek out some green hope, and know that God is a good God of hope and new beginnings.

Dear Lord, thank you that you are the God of green hope. We need hope today—help us to find it in any small way possible. Along with that hope, may we also experience joy and peace in your presence. Amen.

17. Pleading for Us

What shall we say about such wonderful things as these? If God is for us, who can ever be against us? Since he did not spare even his own Son but gave him up for us all, won't he also give us everything else? Who dares accuse us whom God has chosen for his own? No one—for God himself has given us right standing with himself. Who then will condemn us? No one—for Christ Jesus died for us and was raised to life for us, and he is sitting in the place of honor at God's right hand, pleading for us. Can anything ever separate us from Christ's love? Does it mean he no longer loves us if we have trouble or calamity, or are persecuted, or hungry, or destitute, or in danger, or threatened with death? (As the Scriptures say, "For your sake we are killed every day; we are being slaughtered like sheep.) No, despite all these things, overwhelming victory is ours through Christ, who loved us.
—Romans 8:31-37 (NLT)

Sometimes all we can think about is pain, whether emotional or physical. I've had my share of emotional pain, but lately it tips toward the physical. In the times when we are severely hurting, we can do little more than beg for relief.

Last Thursday, I had a migraine. I also felt twinges of bladder pain, but I ignored that because my head was screaming much louder. By Friday, I had constant urinary tract pain. Uh-oh. Then came nausea, fever, increased pain, etc. I used to have UTIs all the time, but I have been blessed with a reprieve for about a year. I had forgotten how life-altering they are. In addition to the pain, nausea, fever, and exhaustion, there's an unsettling, anxious feeling that is just awful. I was pleading for it to stop.

I'm better now (thanks to the antibiotics I didn't want to take but needed), and today I'm a bit more relaxed. I watched a sermon today on the passage from Romans 8, and one thing that stuck out to me is that Jesus is pleading for us right now. Isn't that the sweetest, most beautiful thought? So while you may be begging for relief from whatever problems or pain you're enduring, you have a Savior who is also on your side, pleading for you.

We then go on to read in this passage that no matter what trouble we face, Jesus loves us and nothing can separate us from his love. Overwhelming victory will be ours through Christ. That is comforting in the most expansive way.

Lord Jesus, thank you that you love us always, no matter what we face or what we do. Thank you for pleading for us and sitting with us through the pain. It means everything. Amen.

18. Struggling for Strength

For I can do everything through Christ, who gives me strength. —Philippians 4:13 (NLT)

I really wanted to be strong Sunday, but I woke up with joint pain and nausea. Then a migraine hit me at 9:30 am. and that was about it for the day. Still, I'm not giving up and giving in to these diseases. They will not win.

I missed my Sunday school class, but that's okay. God understood. God was busy giving me strength to make it through the day. Some days, I just have the strength to get through and not much else. Other days, I can manage to check a few things off my list. Which kind of day are you having today?

I firmly believe that God wants me—and you—strong. God doesn't want us sick all the time. Our part in this daily struggle is to do what we can when we can. What can you manage to do for your health today? Maybe all you can do today is eat healthy food, drink plenty of clean water, and stretch in your bed. Maybe tomorrow you can do a load of laundry, take some vitamins, and go for a short walk. Some days, or lots of days, you may have to take medications, even if you really don't want to.

You didn't choose to be sick. It's not all under your control. However, there are some things you can do. Do what you can today, lean into Christ's strength, and work for a better tomorrow.

Dear Lord, thank you for loaning me your strength when I can't seem to find any of my own. Help me to make healthy choices and work to get better. May I feel your presence and know that I'm never alone, no matter how bad the pain gets. Amen.

19. I Hate Technology

Don't worry about anything; instead, pray about every-thing. Tell God what you need, and thank him for all he has done. Then you will experience God's peace, which exceeds anything we can understand. His peace will guard your hearts and minds as you live in Christ Jesus. —Philippians 4:6-7 (NLT)

This week has been a nightmare. Okay, not in a tragic way, but in a "I hate technology and want to throw all the computers out the window" way. It was our first experience with online school. We are at a new online charter school with tons of new software I've never seen, and my printer picked this week to forget how to print and scan. Pages won't load; audio files won't upload; homework won't print or scan. To say that we've been frustrated would be a huge understatement. There have been tears (and not just mine).

The first day I worked on it day and night, having no time for my own work or chores. By the end of the day, I was worried and stressed. How was I going to make this work for my second grader and for me? Did we make a mistake with this type of school? Should I give up now before she's scarred for life?

Also, I had two doctor's appointments this week, with the experts recommending two new controversial treatments and a very expensive out-of-pocket test. I was worried about that, too. Are the treatments safe? Can we afford them? I've tried so many things that it's hard to believe anymore that something might work.

I want you to know that I'm well aware that my worries this week may sound like a summer breeze to you. People are facing so many difficult things as I write this, with layoffs, illness, and political and racial issues. My small concerns are no match for those enormous problems.

However, they matter to me this week, and therefore they matter to God. God's word says to pray about everything and worry about nothing. So that's what I'll do. I'm praying that online school will get easier as I learn the software and that I'll be able to make this a positive experience for my daughter without daily tears. I'm praying for guidance regarding the new treatments and test. I'm praying for patience and enough strength for each day. The more I do this, the more at peace I feel about everything.

God's got this. God's got the small things . . . as well as the enormously devastating things.

Why don't you try giving God your small things and big things?

Dear God, we are overwhelmed with so many things. Help us to remember to talk with you about it. Take our worries and replace them with peace. In Jesus's name, Amen.

20. Know the Real Jesus

Put on your new nature, and be renewed as you learn to know your Creator and become like him. —Colossians 3: 10 (NLT)

I am currently reading a good book by John Eldredge titled *Beautiful Outlaw*. It is about seeking and finding the real Jesus—not the one taught to you by religion but the one you discover for yourself in the Bible. The simple yet profound prayer Eldredge suggests in the book is this: "Jesus, I ask you for you. For the real you."

As I've prayed this prayer, it has forced me to let go of some preconceived notions about Jesus. I've been in church my whole life, and I've been taught some very incorrect things by well-meaning Sunday school teachers. It's not all bad, of course, but it all needs sifting through.

Jesus asks for a personal relationship with us. This requires time, effort, and honesty. It's a real friendship. He already knows the real you, so you can and should be your real self with Jesus.

That means being completely honest about your past and then letting go of it. It means letting all your pain spill out to him, knowing that he won't tire of your whining. It means not being afraid to ask him all the questions.

So today, no matter how you are feeling, just be with Jesus. Discover for yourself who he is. Seek the real Jesus.

Dear Jesus, I ask you for you. For the real you. Amen.

21. Unexpected Delight

May God our Father himself and our Master Jesus clear the road to you! And may the Master pour on the love so it fills your lives and splashes over on everyone around you, just as it does from us to you. May you be infused with strength and purity, filled with confidence in the presence of God our Father when our Master Jesus arrives with all his followers.
—1 Thessalonians 3:11-13 (MSG)

Due to lupus, I can only go for walks when it's cloudy. Most people with lupus/SLE are photosensitive, and the sun makes their symptoms worse. (For me, that sensitivity means nausea, migraines, more pain, and sometimes rashes/hives.) I woke up one morning last week to a cloudy day. I always feel like I've missed my opportunity if I don't walk on a cloudy day, so, despite not feeling well, I made myself go for a short walk in the neighborhood. While walking, I was focused on what joints hurt: my right ankle, my right foot and toes, my left knee, my right hip (new area), my left shoulder, my mid and lower back, my neck, and my head. I can't make this stuff up—it all hurt. I kept wondering why I even bothered to push myself to walk when it was so painful. I wondered how I would get through the day, especially the virtual-schooling part.

Completely ignoring what was around me, I focused on hurting everywhere. I was walking by a wooded area in the back of my neighborhood when, all of a sudden, I was startled by a rustle in the trees. I glanced up to see two deer run deeper into the woods. I laughed and was immediately filled with delight and joy. Suddenly my pain didn't feel so burdensome. Don't get me wrong; my pain didn't go away, but now I could carry it a little lighter.

I gave thanks for that gift. I had never before seen deer in my neighborhood (in nine years of walks), and I needed that unexpected delight at that moment. It felt like God was saying "I love you" and that there was still joy in life.

I am praying that each one of you will feel a moment of unexpected delight this week and, in that moment, experience the love of Jesus Christ surrounding you. I want you to know that I love you, too. That is the reason I started writing devotions. I care about you. I also want you to know that life is not all bad, even when you are hurting everywhere (physically and/or emotionally). There is always hope and love in Christ, and one day you will hurt no longer.

Jesus, help us to lift our heads up from the pain and look around at what you have for us. May we notice you in your creation, and may we allow ourselves to experience the joy in your love. Amen.

22. Just Go Ahead

My counsel for you is simple and straightforward: Just go ahead with what you've been given. You received Christ Jesus, the Master; now live *him. You're deeply rooted in him. You're well-constructed upon him. You know your way around the faith. Now do what you've been taught. School's out; quit studying the subject and start* living *it! And let your living spill over into thanksgiving.* —Colossians 2:6-7 (MSG)

Yesterday, I woke with a headache and felt bad all day. I couldn't play hide-and-seek or dance party like my daughter wanted. I could, however, watch a movie with her. Today, thankfully, I'm better. I was able to do a cooking lesson with her and help her get set up with a lemonade stand. The point is that I do what I can when I can.

What can you do today? Look back at the passage above, which says, "Just go ahead with what you've been given," and then quickly reminds us that we have received the gift of Jesus. It gives me the courage to go ahead and do what I can for the day, knowing that Jesus is with me. I should live out my faith, loving God and others the best that I can. Sometimes that doesn't look like much from the outside, while other times it looks like a lot.

Do you want to know a secret? I don't really care what it looks like from the outside. It's between me and God. I'm done feeling guilty or ashamed about what I can't accomplish when I'm sick. At least, I'm done with that for today.

What can you go ahead with today, knowing that Jesus Christ is with you? Maybe you can't go out for coffee with a friend (because you're sick or because you're isolating due to Covid), but can you write her a letter or text her? Maybe you don't have the energy for roller skating with your son, but can you read a book together? Let's focus on what we *can* do this week rather than what we can't do. Then, let's try to be thankful for whatever it is that we manage to do.

Jesus, thank you for the reminder that you're with us, whether we are able to do much or little today. Help us to have thankful hearts and be able to express our love in tangible ways to those around us. Amen.

23. Not Yet Fully Formed

God is love. When we take up permanent residence in a life of love, we live in God and God lives in us. This way, love has the run of the house, becomes at home and mature in us, so that we're free of worry on Judgment Day—our standing in the world is identical with Christ's. There is no room in love for fear. Well-formed love banishes fear. Since fear is crippling, a fearful life—fear of death, fear of judgment—is one not yet fully formed in love. —1 John 4:17-18 (MSG)

There are all levels of fear. I started a new medication this week that I give myself through daily shots in my stomach. I've often given myself shots in the leg, with a self-injector, for other meds. I was scared, though, about injecting my stomach and using regular syringes. I've never been a fan of blood and needles. However, it's no big deal. There was no reason to fear.

Yesterday, I got the call that my brother has Covid. What's worse is that my parents, both in their late seventies, have been around him. Now I have reason to fear. This is a totally different level of fear. This is the fear I've had since I first learned of this coronavirus. Now, when I pray every day for all the people in the world with disease, it's very personal. My next prayer is always for those who have lost loved ones this year. I definitely don't want that prayer to be personal. No one does. That is where my fear lies today—in death.

Yet I read in 1 John 4 that a "fearful life . . . is one not yet fully formed in love." That's hard to swallow, but I'm sure it's true. I love God. I seek God every day, and I attempt to connect with God, but

I'm not there yet. I still live with fear. Do I think God is aggravated with me that I'm not at that level yet, the level of being fully formed in love? No, I think Jesus is right next to me, understanding my fear, yet trying to calm me and stretch me into a deeper, more peaceful state.

I know many of you have loved ones who are sick right now. If you're reading this, you likely have a chronic illness and are at greater risk of doing poorly if you contract Covid, flu, and a host of other diseases. It's nearly impossible to be fearless. I'm not asking you not to fear. I'm suggesting that you talk to Jesus about it. Ask Jesus to be with you in the fear and guide you to a little more peace. I firmly believe that Jesus will do this for you.

Dear God, we're scared. Sickness is cruel and awful. We pray for an end to it, but for now, please help us walk through the fear every day. Help us to experience your presence while we do the best we can with our emotions. Amen.

24. Convictions of Steel

Every time we think of you, we thank God for you. Day and night you're in our prayers as we call to mind your work of faith, your labor of love, and your patience of hope in following our Master, Jesus Christ, before God our Father. It is clear to us, friends, that God not only loves you very much but also has put his hand on you for something special. When the Message we preached came to you, it wasn't just words. Something happened in you. The Holy Spirit put steel in your convictions. —1 Thessalonians 1:2-5 (MSG)

God has "put his hand on you for something special." Is that comforting to you, or is it daunting? Do you feel blessed by that or stressed? I feel both. Sometimes it's hard to discern what that something special is and whether you are doing it correctly. Sometimes it is more than one thing and it often changes throughout life. "Steel in your convictions" is a strong phrase—it implies real strength in what you are about. What are you firm and sure about? In more common terminology, what are you passionate about?

Here's a look at some of my passions: I am passionate about helping patients as an SLP (speech-language pathologist). I am passionate about educating clinicians to help patients. I am passionate about parenting my children. I am passionate about finding a cure for lupus, arthritis, and so many other chronic conditions. I am passionate about encouraging and giving hope to others with chronic illness. That last passion has led me to you.

My most passionate passion, however, is Jesus Christ. I am passionate about following him, knowing him, and helping others to know him. That's also what led me to you.

I pray that you have found a passion or two (or six). If not, keep looking and searching. I believe that God has something special for you to do. You are not too sick or too weak to have convictions of steel. You just need a little hope to keep going and keep seeking. In the meantime, look to Jesus. Seek him, and he will lead you to your convictions of steel.

Lord Jesus, help me discover the convictions of steel that you have placed in my heart. Give me the hope and strength needed each day to pursue them. I want to do something special for you. Thank you for loving me so very much. Amen.

25. Love and Endurance

May the Master take you by the hand and lead you along the path of God's love and Christ's endurance.
—2 Thessalonians 3:5 (MSG)

This is a short verse, but, oh, how I love it! It packs so much into one sentence. First, I love the imagery of the Master taking me by the hand. Think of the power of holding hands. How does it feel when a newborn wraps their tiny hand around your finger?

My oldest daughter used to hold my hand while rubbing my thumbnail. It was so comforting to her. If I had nail polish on, she would get agitated, so I went years with bare nails for her. She's sixteen now, so that little routine is long over! Now, however, when I hold hands with my younger daughter or my husband, I feel an almost instant exhalation of stress. Does hand-holding affect you that way? When I think of Jesus holding my hand and walking with me, it is so comforting that it gives me the strength to endure illness, pain, a pandemic, fear, and anything else life throws at me this week.

Another key to survival is in the second part of 2 Thessalonians 3:5. With "God's love" and "Christ's endurance," we can get through this (whatever this is). He will lead us when we can't take the next step or even the next breath. Christ will endure it or suffer it with us while we are bathed in God's love. These are the two key elements, then, that we need to survive and thrive in this life: love and endurance. These gifts are freely ours.

Remember how you used to feel when holding your grandmother's hand or your mother's hand or the hand of anyone you loved deeply and felt safe with? I hope and pray that there was someone like that for you. Imagine that comforting, love-filled feeling with Jesus holding your hand.

Now you know you can make it. You can do this—together with Jesus.

Jesus, thank you for always enduring with me and always holding my hand in love. Amen.

26. Speak Encouragement

So speak encouraging words to one another. Build up hope so you'll all be together in this, no one left out, no one left behind. I know you're already doing this; just keep on doing it. —1 Thessalonians 5:11 (MSG)

In my part of the country this week, we had a major ice storm. All the trees were covered in thick ice, with branches drooping and whole trees lost. Many people lost power, and some had home and car damage (not to mention fences). In the midst of this, one person we know had a house fire. In other parts of the country, there are fires and hurricanes. It often feels like we have entirely too much too deal with!.

I teach college online. I have one student whose whole family has Covid. I have another student whose mother is extremely ill. I have many students who emailed me this week saying they have no power and can't do their assignments. (Yes, of course, I gave them all extensions—I'm not a monster!) I was wondering, though, what more I could do to help them. What can I do from a computer, some distance away? I can encourage them through e-mails and posts. I can try to keep some semblance of normalcy as I teach and interact with them each week.

Life is hard right now—for everyone. I know it's extra hard for you as you struggle with pain and illness every single day. I want to encourage you today with some simple truths.

- You are loved (John 3:16).
- You are valuable.
- You are special in many very good ways.
- You have a purpose.
- You don't have to be that strong.
- You are never alone.
- You will not always hurt.
- There are still good people in the world.
- You can make a difference, even if you're very sick.
- There are people who care about you, even if you can't see their faces.
- This time of your life, however hard, will not last forever.

These are not fancy words. They don't need to be.

Try to sit still with those truths. I pray that you will be encouraged.

Father God, everything is overwhelming right now. Please help us cling to truth. Help us encourage each other, as we're all together in this life. Amen.

27. Prayerful Preparation

The first thing I want you to do is pray. Pray every way you know how, for everyone you know. Pray especially for rulers and their governments to rule well so we can be quietly about our business of living simply, in humble contemplation. This is the way our Savior God wants us to live. —1 Timothy 2:1-3 (MSG)

I don't think I know anyone who wants to relive the year 2020. It was scary, exhausting, frustrating, isolating, and devastating to so many people. In the introduction, I shared with you what a horrible year 2007 was for me. As I was reading the Bible this week, I thought about 1 Timothy 2:1-3 in regard to looking past difficult years or seasons. What do you do at the beginning of each year? How can we prepare for a new, better year or season of life?

According to 1 Timothy, we can pray—about everything and everyone. We can also simplify our lives, be humble, and spend time in prayerful contemplation. A lot of people I know took time during the pandemic to examine their lives, thinking about what activities and material possessions they could eliminate. I don't know about you, but I cleaned out every closet and drawer in my house! Have you considered what is in your life right now that doesn't need to be?

I think being humble is a prerequisite to meaningful prayer. We must acknowledge that God is God, and without God we are nothing. Most of us know that prayer is simply talking to God. We can pray for our world, for our country, for those who are sick or hurt or hungry, for our families and friends, and for our own needs, health, and worries. We can, and should, praise God for who God is and ask for forgiveness. We should also be thankful for our many blessings, large and small. Prayer needs no ending. It can be continuous, throughout the day.

What about contemplation? Wikipedia says that contemplation has been described as "a gaze of faith, a silent love." Isn't that beautiful? We can be still, gaze at Jesus, and silently listen in love. I have a close friend who introduced me to the idea of "contemplative prayer" a couple of years ago. Since then, I have practiced the discipline of being quiet and listening to God. I am still not good at it, as I can't seem to tame my intrusive thoughts, but I keep trying. When I get it right, it is glorious—peaceful and fulfilling like nothing else I've ever known. I highly recommend that you give it a try or, rather, many tries.

If you're going through a difficult season of life, take the time to prepare your heart for something better. Remember that you can pray about everything; think about what you don't need in your life; practice humility; and take time to listen for God's sweet, soft voice.

God, help me to humble myself before you and pray about everyone and everything, all day long. Help me to simplify my life and discipline myself to be quiet and listen to you. Amen.

28. Spiritual Exercise

You've been raised on the Message of the faith and have followed sound teaching. Now pass on this counsel to the followers of Jesus there, and you'll be a good servant of Jesus. Stay clear of silly stories that get dressed up as religion. Exercise daily in God—no spiritual flabbiness, please! Workouts at the gymnasium are useful, but a disciplined life in God is far more so, making you fit both today and forever. You can count on this. Take it to heart. This is why we've thrown ourselves into this venture so totally. We're banking on the living God, Savior of all men and women, especially believers. —1 Timothy 4:7-10 (MSG)

Due to persistent intestinal permeability, dysbiosis, and ulcerative colitis, my doctor and dietician decided I needed to go on a liquid elemental diet for five days this week. That was five days of choking down a disgusting smoothie three times a day, with exhaustion, nausea, stomach cramps, and more. It was hard. I certainly didn't feel like exercising, but I forced myself to do stretching and gentle yoga each day. Why would I do that to myself? I have learned over time that if I take a break from all exercise, then my arthritis gets worse with more pain and stiffness.

This is similar in some ways to my time with God. If I skip a day of prayer, Bible reading, and quiet listening, then I am not the person I want to be. My day usually is more of a struggle, with increased frustration and less peace. Have you noticed this, too? Maybe you can't spend thirty minutes with God today, but how about two minutes? I understand that some days you might not be able to think clearly enough to attend a Bible study or feel well enough even to concentrate on reading a chapter of the Bible. Could you utter a verse that you have memorized and mediate on that? Could you pray, really pray, the Lord's Prayer? Could you whisper a short "Help me, Lord, I love you" prayer? Some days, that can be enough.

Lord God, we know we need time with you today. Why, then, do we put it off? Forgive us, please, and nudge us towards you. Help us do more than just survive the day. Amen.

29. Calm and Delight

Your God is present among you, a strong Warrior there to save you. Happy to have you back, he'll calm you with his love and delight you with his songs. —Zephaniah 3:17 (MSG)

Calm and delight—that sounds like exactly what I need right now. How about you? As I write, Covid-19 cases are approaching 200,000 per day. Half of the country thinks we have a new president and half of the country thinks we don't. It seems like everyone is angry. We can't (or aren't supposed to) see our relatives and friends for Thanksgiving and Christmas. Could life be more of a bummer right now? Oh, sure it could: just add daily pain and sickness from chronic illness.

Right now, I am literally trying not to throw up (daily nausea), and my neck, back, and hip are throbbing (arthritis). I am so sad about the holidays, as I miss my aunts, uncles, and cousins whom I haven't seen since last Christmas (since Easter was also cancelled). My teenage daughter thinks she was exposed yesterday, so she can't return home today, since I'm very "high risk." Yet, in my whining, I know that I am one of the fortunate ones. I have not yet lost a family member to the coronavirus. My husband and I still have jobs. I have everything I need, and I really have no reason to complain.

As I go to God and confess my whining amid so much suffering in the world, I feel heavy and burdened. Yet God leads me to this verse of calm and delight. I slowly try to relax and look around me at what I can "delight" in—like the fact that I have a little time to read today or that I just received a hug from my younger daughter. Despite all the suffering in the world, God is here among us. God is trying to calm us if we will just be still, breathe, and take God's hand. God is also trying to provide us with little moments of joy and delight amid all the chaos and despair. It is okay to notice those positive moments and enjoy them. It is even okay to seek them out. So today I will go smell the only remaining rose in my backyard that hasn't received the message of winter. I will be still and be with God for a while. I will play some uplifting music, and I will wrap some Christmas presents. I will seek calm and delight because I really need them. Don't you?

God, the whole world seems depressed right now. We feel heavy and burdened. May each of us find some moments of calm and delight this week. Thank you for providing those things right when we need them. Thank you for your unique ability to calm us and delight us. Amen.

30. Those Crooked People

Do everything without complaining and arguing, so that no one can criticize you. Live clean, innocent lives as children of God, shining like bright lights in a world full of crooked and perverse people. Hold firmly to the word of life. —Philippians 2:14-16a (NLT)

I watched the news this morning. It's not like I needed a reminder that the world is full of crooked and perverse people. I recognize that almost all the time. Don't you? There's bad news everywhere, and sometimes it seems like most people are untrustworthy and evil. Everyone is fighting and arguing. Haven't you felt that even more the last few years?

Then, I pray and confess my sins, and I am convicted that maybe I'm a little bent myself. Maybe I'm the one complaining and arguing. Am I doing my part in being the bright light? Remember the verse about removing the plank in your own eye (Matt 7:5)? That verse is hard to swallow, yet it is so true. I need to work on myself and quit blaming those other people for the state of the world.

This is not easy work. The key, I believe, is in the verse found before the above passage: "For God is working in you, giving you the desire and the power to do what pleases him" (Phil 2:13). If I don't like who I'm being lately, then I am not spending enough time with God. If I discipline myself to be with God, then God will give me the desire and ability to shine brighter in the world.

Today I am spending more time with God. I am going to hold my tongue and refuse to argue about politics. I'm going to choose to focus on my blessings (Jesus, family, food, job) rather than my complaints (new medicine side effects, chronic illness, pandemic). I'm going to be kind and try to shine. I will fail, I'm sure, but tomorrow I will try again.

God, when we're honest, we know that we are part of the problem. Help us to focus on you this week. Help us become brighter lights in the world, choosing hope over despair. Even though there's little evidence of it, that is truly our hearts' desire. Please help us be better. Amen.

31. The Most Capable Coworker

This is the Message I've been set apart to proclaim as preacher, emissary, and teacher. It's also the cause of all this trouble I'm in. But I have no regrets. I couldn't be more sure of my ground—the One I've trusted in can take care of what he's trusted me to do right to the end. —2 Timothy 1:11-12 (MSG)

My sixteen-year-old daughter went to her dad's house for the weekend before Thanksgiving. She just got back, twelve days later. She missed Thanksgiving and she missed school. Many of you can relate, I'm sure. She was exposed to Covid in her dad's house, and everyone there got sick. At first, I thought she was going to have a light case, but then she got really sick—too sick to move from her bed, she said. As a mom, I felt panicked and helpless. I couldn't take care of her, and I couldn't be sure that someone else was taking care of her. I prayed and prayed and asked others to pray, and I lived for text and phone call updates for a few days. Thankfully, she didn't end up in the hospital, as so many are now, and she is recovering.

My point is that God entrusted me to take care of my daughters. At a time when I couldn't do that directly, God took care of her for me, just as 2 Timothy 1:12 says. As I look back, I realize that God has been doing that her whole life, since she was three and her dad and I divorced, throughout all the visitation periods. That's the most reassuring thing about our work here on earth. We are not alone in this work—big or small!

Last week, when I was getting frustrated trying to teach my eight-year-old to "borrow" in subtraction, God was there in that tiny moment, helping us through it. I am currently trying to figure out how to encourage my online college students to persist in their degree, despite their overwhelming challenges. Some of them want to give up, as life is so hard for everyone right now, and school seems like one thing too many. I know that God will give me the words to type or to say.

I know some of you are currently in such physical pain that you think you can't make it through this day. I understand that. I want to encourage you to breathe and to pray to God for help. Ask God to give you the strength to endure and to do whatever is absolutely necessary today, and then leave the rest for tomorrow. This past week, I had four migraine days. Those four days I was unable to cook, do chores, grade papers, etc. My younger daughter basically had to entertain herself while my husband was at work. The laundry and other chores didn't get done, and my daughter had too much screen time, but it all basically worked out. As you know, life doesn't go the way we plan it out. Yes, we have work to do, but when we can't do it, God will make a way. When we are able to do the work, God is working right alongside us. We can relax knowing that we are never alone in our work. In fact, we have the most capable coworker ever!

Thank you, God, that you work alongside us and for us. Give us strength to do what we can, yet give us hope and reassurance that you've got it all under control when we can't complete our work for the day. Help us endure, Lord, through these difficult days. Amen.

32. There's Nothing Like the Word

There's nothing like the written Word of God for showing you the way to salvation through faith in Christ Jesus. Every part of Scripture is God-breathed and useful one way or another—showing us truth, exposing our rebellion, correcting our mistakes, training us to live God's way. Through the Word we are put together and shaped up for the tasks God has for us. —2 Timothy 3:15-17 (MSG)

If you feel lost, confused, discouraged, convicted, or useless today, read the Bible. God speaks to us through this word. Jesus, the Word, the Life, the Light, and the Truth, works through us as we read, study, and contemplate. The Spirit of God moves our thoughts in a certain direction. The next time we read the same passage, our thoughts may veer in a different direction. At least, that is how it seems to work for me.

Throughout my life, I've found value in the word of God, no matter how I'm feeling or what is happening to me or around me. When going through betrayal and divorce, the Psalms were helpful for expressing my anger and devastation. They validated my feelings and made me realize that I was not the first (or the last) to experience that kind of despair.

When trudging through daily life with chronic illness, I have found encouragement that this suffering will not continue forever. Someday, as the Bible reminds us, we won't be in any pain at all. In addition, the Bible tells us that we are learning and growing through such trials. Thus, maybe the pain and sickness are not a useless waste after all. I'm gaining some benefit, although it is nearly impossible to see.

When I feel unloved, the Bible reminds me again and again how much God loved us. God gave God's one and only Son for us. God gave everything. God loves us despite ourselves.

When I feel useless in comparison to the "successful people" of the world, God's word reminds me what is truly valuable to God. We can simply be quiet and spend time with God, and that is success in God's eyes.

When I feel discouraged about the state of violence, betrayal, hatred, and injustice in the world, I find peace in the Bible. The word of God tells us that this horrid state is not the end. One day, everything will be alright. One day, Jesus Christ will reign. In the meantime, however, we can do our part to be a light in the world.

No matter what you're feeling today, open the word of God. It is not only comforting and encouraging, but it is useful. "Through the Word we are put together and shaped up for the tasks God has for us." If you're feeling overwhelmed, pulled apart, and out of shape, go to the word.

Heavenly Father, thank you for your word. Thank you for all you provide to us through the Bible. Help us to pause, read, pray, and think. Help us to spend more time with you. Amen.

33. Joyless Christmas?

Always be joyful. Always keep on praying. No matter what happens, always be thankful, for this is God's will for you who belong to Christ. —1 Thessalonians 5:16-18 (NLT)

Suddenly an angel of the Lord appeared among them, and the radiance of the Lord's glory surrounded them. They were terrified, but the angel reassured them. "Don't be afraid!" he said. "I bring you good news that will bring great joy to all people. The Savior—yes, the Messiah, the Lord—has been born today in Bethlehem, the city of David! And you will recognize him by this sign: You will find a baby wrapped snugly in strips of cloth, lying in a manger. —Luke 2:9-12 (NLT)

Usually when I read the Christmas story about Jesus in a manger, I am filled with a sense of peace and joy. The thought that God, the Creator of everything, would be humble enough to become human fills me with both awe and thankfulness. Sometimes, however, the tragedies and disappointments of life tend to cloud the joy of Christmas. It's hard to be joyful when you've lost a loved one in the past year. It's hard to be joyful when you are worried about a virus or the flu, which can both be deadly for people with compromised immune systems. It's hard to be joyful when you are suffering from a chronic illness. It was hard to be joyful during Christmas 2020, when we couldn't be with our families for Christmas due to the pandemic.

I am reminded of a miserable Christmas Eve in 2009. I was a divorced single parent, awaiting the arrival of my five-year-old daughter home that evening. We had a "standard visitation schedule," which meant that one year she would come home Christmas Eve and be with me until school started back, and the next year she would leave for her dad's on Christmas Eve and be gone until school started back after the new year. I preferred the years she came home on Christmas Eve, of course, because then we could wake up together on Christmas morning, with all the joy of both Jesus and Santa Claus. On this particular Christmas Eve, however, the meteorologists knew early in the morning that a winter storm was coming. I called my ex-husband, begging him to let her come home early before the storm hit. He refused. As predicted, the storm hit, and he would not get out and bring her home. My daughter and I missed Christmas Eve *and* Christmas morning together. To say I was disappointed would be a dramatic understatement. I was downright depressed. Looking to the past and the future, I realized that this meant I would miss three years—three Christmas mornings in a row (at ages four, five, and six). All parents know how precious and limited those times are, since children too quickly outgrow the magic. I went to bed that night crying, alone, praying to God in desperation, and mourning lost Christmas joy. I tossed and turned all night in my misery.

To my surprise, however, I woke the next morning with a lighter heart in a sunny room. I immediately read Luke 2 in my Bible. I prayed and thought, "My daughter is not with me, but Jesus is. He is born, so let's go celebrate!" My transformation was almost miraculous and can only be attributed to God's work. I went to bed a miserable creature but woke up to light and joy. Was I still sad? Yes, but the joy was greater than the sadness. Perhaps that's the point: the joy of Jesus can outshine any and all of our sadness.

If you have ever had a miserable Christmas or are honestly dreading the next one, my humble advice is to cry out to God in your despair. List all your complaints, feelings, and pain, and confess that you are unable to find the joy in Jesus's birth this year. Then, sit with God, try to rest, read the Christmas story, and search deep in your soul for a little spark of joy.

Lord, life is just miserable sometimes, even at Christmas. We want to be joyful, but we are hurting, desperate, and disappointed. Lead us, Jesus, into the light of your joy this week. We truly want to seek and celebrate you. Amen.

34. Go to the Psalms

Save me, O God, for the floodwaters are up to my neck.
—Psalm 69:1

Turn us again to yourself, O God. Make your face shine down upon us. Only then will we be saved. —Psalm 80:3

O God, do not be silent! —Psalm 83:1 (NLT)

As I write this, another week has passed in the United States, but not without setting yet another record of the most Covid deaths in one day as well as bringing us the divisive storming of our nation's Capitol (January 6, 2021). Maybe you have suffered with Covid, or a family member has suffered or passed from it. Maybe you are concerned about the divisiveness in our society and worried about our nation's future. Maybe you are just struggling to get out of bed today, overwhelmed with physical pain and weakness. For nearly everyone I know, life is hard to take right now.

My advice is to turn to the Psalms to help with your prayers. First, cry out to God—the Psalms can help you express your anger, your struggle, your hurt. Do not hesitate to cry or scream out what you feel and think. God will not be offended. God made you; Jesus lived on this earth; Jesus understands and cries with you. Cry out, as in Psalm 69: "Save me!"

What can you do after laying your heart out on the table, leaving nothing unsaid to God? You can pray, as in Psalm 80 above, that God will help you turn fully back to God. Search your own heart to see what you need to do right now in order to turn your life more fully to God.

Third, stop and listen to God. We can certainly plead along with the psalmist in Psalm 83 for God to "not be silent," but then we must listen for God to speak. You can't listen if you don't stop talking. Take time to listen. You must intentionally focus on listening. This is difficult for us, and it requires lots of practice.

Today, if you're feeling depressed about your illness or your marriage or the state of our nation, if you're angry and grieving, or if you're just plain sick of being sick all the time, start with a cry to God. Examine your life and which way(s) you need to turn. Last, just stop and listen. I sincerely hope and pray that the Psalms will bring you some peace this week.

Holy God, life feels bad and overwhelming. Please listen to my feelings and my complaints. Lord, I am hurt. I am sad. I am discouraged. Nudge me in the right direction, and help me to be open to your whispers. In Jesus's name, Amen.

35. Whatever You Do or Say

And whatever you do or say, do it as a representative of the Lord Jesus, giving thanks through him to God the Father.
—Colossians 3:17 (NLT)

This verse is extremely special to me. It was included in a bigger passage that my husband and I chose for our wedding. We later chose this one verse as the "life verse" for my youngest daughter at her baby dedication. Recently, we reminded her of this verse at her baptism. We chose Colossians 3:17 because we think it is a good way to live life. As Christians, it is our job to represent Christ to the rest of the world in everything we say and do. The second part of the verse reminds us that we are called to be thankful and to praise God, no matter what is going on. Not only is this a sign of obedience, but thanking God for our many blessings (even in the midst of difficulty) can enrich our lives.

I invite you to think through all the jobs you have had. How did you represent Christ through each of them? How could you have done this better? How can you represent Christ more completely in what you say and do this week? Here are a few examples from my life to get you thinking. When I worked at a tutoring center as a teenager, I represented Christ, at least most of the time, through the patience I needed to have with those children. For example, I remember working over and over with an intellectually challenged teenager, older than I was at the time, on how to utilize a calculator for basic math. We would do the same thing each week, and he would make progress, but by the next week everything was mostly forgotten. I was usually patient, at least on the outside. However, I think I let my pride get the best of me sometimes as I thought how great it was that I could help someone older than me.

As a young professional speech-language pathologist, I thought I knew exactly what my clients needed. I was determined that they would succeed. I thought I knew the best way for them to improve quickly, and that was with the help of their parents doing daily speech drills with them. Now I see that I lacked empathy and understanding for those parents, as I would become angry at them for not practicing with their children, thinking that they didn't really care. Once I became a parent myself, I realized how overwhelming it is. Some of those parents were just trying to get food on the table and the rent paid. They were in survival mode and didn't have time for my "speech practice." I learned to adapt the homework into something that the parents were already doing, teaching them how to practice while driving to school or while giving the child a bath. This didn't add much extra work to their already overwhelming to-do list, and the parents were more likely to get it done. Most parents want to help their children succeed; you just have to find out how to help them work it into their lives.

Today, I struggle with empathy for the college students I teach who do not get their assignments in on time. I struggle with patience as I work on reading comprehension with my home-schooled daughter. I struggle with love and understanding for my family members who are so politically extreme. My point is that I always struggle, yet I still try to represent Christ. Thankfully, I get a new day today to try again.

Dear Lord, help us to represent you better to others in all that we do and say. We fail daily, but we keep trying. Thank you for new days and new beginnings. Help us also to notice our blessings today, as such thankfulness renews our souls. Amen.

36. Grab the Promised Hope

We who have run for our very lives to God have every reason to grab the promised hope with both hands and never let go. It's an unbreakable spiritual lifeline, reaching past all appearances right to the very presence of God where Jesus, running on ahead of us, has taken up the permanent post as high priest for us, in the order of Melchizedek. —Hebrews 6:18-20 (MSG)

I've had pain in my left ankle since 2010. Every morning, when I first wake up, I'm very aware of the fact that my ankle is so stiff it won't move. As I try and try to work it free, I feel excruciating pain. It gradually lessens, and then it's mostly okay for the rest of the day.

A couple of months ago, I tried a new, somewhat experimental treatment for my arthritis. In the last two weeks, when I wake up, I don't even feel that ankle. It's absolutely amazing to me—I had completely forgotten what waking up with a normal ankle felt like! There's no placebo effect here, I assure you, because I never expected this. This new development has given me a bit of hope that I can get better and actually improve my health. Hope is freeing, liberating, and fresh, leaving the stale air of despair and monotony behind. When you're chronically sick, with every day feeling like the same desperate struggle, it can be hard to hold on to hope for health.

This week, I also have hope for our divided country. A "Celebrating America" special I watched last night highlighted generous Americans and how they are helping each other through dark times. It was inspiring and hopeful. It reminded me of a saying I heard the other day on the radio, which was, "the world is full of nice people, but, if you can't find one, then be one."

Now I realize that you may be in a very different place today. Maybe you can't get out of bed, suffering with pain or nausea or fever. Maybe you're not hopeful for the state of the world or ever feeling better. I want you to know that you still have available to you the unshakeable, "unbreakable spiritual lifeline" of God. God is the source of our greatest eternal hope. This is huge hope, far bigger than medical symptoms or earthly things. God is waiting to give you hope today. Run to God; spend time with God; cry out to God; be still and listen. Then, grab God's "promised hope" with all the strength you have left.

Dear God, it's hard to be hopeful in our world. It's hard to keep going sometimes. Please bring sparks of hope into our lives so that we may become aware of your presence. Remind us that you promise something much greater than all this. Help us to grab your promised hope. In Jesus's name, Amen.

37. Containers

> *In a well-furnished kitchen there are not only crystal goblets and silver platters, but waste cans and compost buckets— some containers used to serve fine meals, others to take out the garbage. Become the kind of container God can use to present any and every kind of gift to his guests for their blessing.* —2 Timothy 2:20-21 (MSG)

I wouldn't say I have a "well-furnished kitchen," but I am certainly overly blessed in what it contains. In fact, I have such an abundance of food in my pantry that I must confess I don't always know what is in there. I had my eight-year-old daughter clean out the pantry yesterday. This seemed like a good idea at the time, but this morning I realized that I don't know where anything is, so it will take me twice as long to cook next week! However, in that process, we found some "surprise" food hidden in the back. In addition, we discovered large serving dishes and a wok. Who knew? I could have been using those containers the last five years, but I obviously hadn't. Now, I can dust them off and put them to use.

In thinking about the verses from 2 Timothy 2, I wonder if I need more flexibility. Am I always the same kind of container for God? Am I always a plain white bowl or a regular glass pie plate? I know I'm not a crystal goblet, but I sure hope I'm not the garbage can! Seriously, though, I'm pretty routine-oriented and stuck in my personality most days. This makes me wonder if God is calling me to stretch myself to utilize various gifts or possibly to utilize the same gifts in various ways. For a clue to what gifts verse 21 means, look ahead to verse 22: "Run away from infantile indulgence. Run after mature righteousness—faith, love, peace—joining those who are in honest and serious prayer before God" (2 Tim 2:22). We're talking about "fruit of the Spirit" kinds of gifts! These are gifts that come from time spent with God.

I'm fairly good with giving the gifts of encouragement and love, at least to my close friends and family. However, I'm not always great with patience. Also, I know that I could stand to dole out more kindness this week. I see that, once again, the key to all of this is prayer. How can I become a new kind of container or vessel for God so that God may bless others through me? How can I stretch myself? I can't do this alone. I must submit to God and then discipline myself to daily "honest and serious prayer." If you're like me and you feel convicted that you're stuck as a sugar bowl most of the time when you should become a canister occasionally, ask God what kind of container you need to be this week. Be willing to accept God's answer.

Dear Lord, we confess that we get stuck in our same old roles or containers, offering up the same gifts day after day. Help us to grow, Lord. Help us to morph into new kinds of containers for you so that we may spill out the types of blessings that are most needed. Amen.

38. Here Are Today's Three Assignments

But for right now, until that completeness, we have three things to do to lead us toward that consummation: Trust steadily in God, hope unswervingly, love extravagantly.
—1 Corinthians 13:13 (MSG)

I teach college, so I think in terms of assignments. What assignments do I have to grade? How many assignments are due this week? Who turned in that assignment late? The last course I taught was different from any I have taught in the last ten years, due to the fact that two students didn't complete the course on time. We got to midterm, and they had turned in absolutely nothing. This was a first for me. To be honest, I was a little panicked (for them and for me). This wasn't due to laziness or procrastination, though, as you might suspect. It was due to Covid. One student had a family member who was extremely ill, and the other student was sick in the hospital herself. They wanted to know if I could give them an extension on the whole course, which meant grading during my Christmas break. Of course I gave it to them. No one asked for this pandemic; it has interrupted almost everything! They were both able to complete the course, thankfully, a month after it concluded, and they continued in the program toward graduation. I admire their tenacity in pushing past such obstacles toward their goals.

When reading 1 Corinthians 13:13, I see three assignments: (1) Trust steadily in God; (2) Hope unswervingly; (3) Love extravagantly. These are recurring assignments. You must do them daily; you're not done until the course of life ends, and, I suspect, you're not done even then. Despite practicing these assignments over and over, however, I am not great at any of them. Some days, I might be nauseous and weak or consumed with arthritis pain, and I begin to lose hope. Other days, I might be too self-focused and forget to love others extravagantly. Maybe I don't understand what is going on with this crazy messed-up world, and I start to lose my trust. God doesn't expect perfection, but I think God does expect tenacity or persistence in our work on these three assignments. I think God also expects progress, no matter how minute.

Notice the word "consummation" in the verse. The sentence prior to this talks about a "completeness" that we're working toward. Verse 12 talks about how we can't see things clearly now, but someday we will. We are working toward something much larger than our tiny personal world, and we are working for the Creator of all. Even though the world makes very little sense sometimes, we still have work to do. If we don't know where to start on a given day, we can simply fall back on these three assignments.

You don't need to have it all together in order to work on these assignments. You can be sick and still work on them. You can be out of a job and still work on them. You can be lonely and still work on them. All that's required is a willing heart and time with Jesus. What are you waiting for? You have three assignments to do!

Lord, I confess that my assignments are not "A"-level work, and I am often frustrated with my progress. Help me to persevere in my daily work. Through daily time with you, please help me with the hard work of faith, hope, and love. Amen.

39. Complaining Is a Sin? Guilty!

Do everything without complaining and arguing, so that no one can criticize you. —Philippians 2:14 (NLT)

Do everything readily and cheerfully—no bickering, no second-guessing allowed! —Philippians 2:14 (MSG)

Last week, my husband and I were doing a children's devotion at bedtime with our eight-year-old daughter. It was about the Israelites and how they kept grumbling and complaining, even after God saved them from slavery, parted the Red Sea for them, and rained down manna for them to eat. The devotion made clear that God considered their complaining to be a sin. We asked our daughter what she complains about and the obvious answer was schoolwork. This is an everyday thing. She has been home for the entire year with me, and every day is a significant struggle with schoolwork. Is she the only one complaining about it? No, I'm just as guilty. I never planned to homeschool, and I haven't been that pleased with it (to put it lightly). In reality, if my own attitude improved, I'm sure it would be more pleasant for both of us. When was the last time I approached the day "readily and cheerfully"?

The fact that complaining is a sin slapped me in the face. Have you ever grown so accustomed to complaining that you don't even think about it? Who hasn't complained about something this week? Everyone is doing it. Not only do I complain about having to teach my own child what an adverb is or how a timeline works, but I frequently complain about not getting to go on vacation enough. "When can

I go back to the beach?" I wail. My husband complains about work. My teenager complains about people whose political beliefs differ from hers. This morning, we were *all* complaining about the ten-degree temperature. We're all a bunch of whiners, now that I think about it, because isn't complaining just a form of whining?

Complaining is expected in our society. If you call a friend, don't you immediately take turns sharing your woes? This situation is driving me crazy. Another appliance in my house broke. Work was too hard this week. My child/spouse/pet did a certain annoying thing. Nothing is going right. Sometimes it seems like a sort of backwards competition to see who has the worst life at the moment. These conversations can go back and forth for hours as we share everything wrong with life. Why are we like this? Why do we *choose* this? As "shining, bright lights" for Christ (read on in Philippians), shouldn't we throw some positive light into all that dark complaining?

Since this book is targeted to people with chronic illness, I'm sure you can also relate to complaining about your symptoms. I feel that I have a lot to choose from with varying diseases, and I'm sure you can relate: my head hurts; my knee is stiff; I'm dizzy; I'm exhausted today; I'm nauseous; etc. Honestly, most of this type of complaining is done inside my head. I try not to complain about my symptoms out loud too much, unless my husband or parents sincerely ask. However, complaining in my head is not good, either. It negatively affects my mindset. Instead of thinking that my foot hurts every time I walk, I could be thankful that I can still walk. Instead of complaining about my restricted diet, I could be thankful that I have good, wholesome food in my refrigerator. Instead of complaining that I've been stuck in my hometown for a year with no vacations, I could be thankful that I haven't been sick with Covid or flu this year. We can't be full of complaints and gratitude at the same time. We choose.

What happens in our heads (complaint versus gratitude) spills out into our words and lives. Often, we live our lives on autopilot, not only not thinking about what we're doing but also not thinking about what or how we're thinking. I believe that if we concentrate on this and prioritize thankfulness in our lives, then we can gradually change our thought patterns into something more positive. It takes discipline to get in the habit of being thankful, but I believe the work is worth it. It might even make us feel better, too. Just do a search for "studies on gratitude" and you will see that research studies have found repeatedly that those who are intentionally thankful each day are happier people. The Bible says, "Rejoice always, pray continually, give thanks in all circumstances, for this is God's will for you in Christ Jesus" (1 Thess 5:16-18). Join me in trying to break the pandemic and practice being thankful rather than complaining.

Heavenly Father, forgive our grumbling. You give us so much, and we're all just a bunch of whiners. We're sorry and we want to do better. Please help us to examine our complaint-filled thoughts and sprinkle in more and more gratitude each day. Thank you for your patience and forgiveness. Amen.

40. What Can You Give Away Today?

This most generous God who gives seed to the farmer that becomes bread for your meals is more than extravagant with you. He gives you something you can then give away, which grows into full-formed lives, robust in God, wealthy in every way, so that you can be generous in every way, producing with us great praise to God. —2 Corinthians 9:10-11 (MSG)

Would you choose to be chronically ill? Would you choose a painful marriage or divorce? Would you choose abuse? I've personally experienced all these things, but I certainly wouldn't have chosen those paths. Sometimes life experiences are terrible or painful or traumatic (or all three), but we can not only learn from them but also help others as a result of them. I think we are called to help others through our ability to empathize from a place of our own pain. The verse above says that God "gives you something you can then give away."

Don't misunderstand me. I don't think God made you chronically ill so that you could suffer. God did not cause someone to abuse you. That's due to the sin of the world—not to God. What I'm saying is that you can be blessed through your negative experiences. Within your healing, you can advance to a new level of knowing God or a new level of connection or a new appreciation of life. Then, you can use this healthier place to help others. You understand their pain because you've been there, and that helps an individual open up to talk to you. In my experience, people are more inclined to talk to those who they think can truly understand their suffering. You might just provide an hour of attentive listening, or you may be able to help walk them through the pain into a blessed healing space. If they have questions, you can answer them, but, mostly, you just listen. God does the healing.

What does "giving away" look like in real life? Everyone has a separate set of experiences to give from. I can understand chronic illness. When I come across someone who is newly diagnosed with a disease or going through a particularly rough patch, I try to listen and provide support for them. As a result of my story, they know I come from a place of understanding the monotony of daily suffering. I try to provide some hope to them, as is my prayer with this book.

When my cousin was divorced several years after my own divorce, under similar circumstances, I was ready to listen, support, and empathize with her. I tried to offer encouragement and hope, with a little bit of advice thrown in. I wanted her to benefit from what I had suffered. I wanted it to be easier for her than it had been for me. There is something wonderful that happens with this "giving away" from your own pain. It's difficult to describe, but it's beautiful and freeing. Your own burden gets a bit lighter and your own pain seems to have more meaning. Painful memories of any type are easier to take if there's meaning behind them. You can say to yourself, "Yes, that was very hard to endure, but now I can help someone through the same situation." Your suffering was not meaningless after all. Be generous, then, with your pain. Don't hoard all those awful memories. If you can choose to share a few of them with someone who is suffering, it may benefit both of you.

Heavenly Father, life is so painful that we often don't want to talk about it. Help me to realize that my painful experiences can be a blessing to me (eventually), as well as to someone else. Provide meaning for my pain by enabling me with the strength to reach out and offer to listen and support others. Amen.

41. Abundantly Free in the Sun (and the Son)

Because of the sacrifice of the Messiah, his blood poured out on the altar of the Cross, we're a free people—free of penalties and punishments chalked up by all our misdeeds. And not just barely free, either. Abundantly free! —Ephesians 1:7-8 (MSG)

As a young child, I remember reading a story about a little girl who was so allergic to the sun that she couldn't play outside. I was horrified by that thought because I loved the sun so much. I loved playing in the sun, and I loved lying in the sun. As a teenager, my nickname became "the lizard" among my friends because I would lie in the sun indefinitely while they played in the water. I remember feeling the rays soaking slowly into my skin, and I would get this delicious, shivery feeling of freedom and warmth. Have you felt this? I hope so because it is one of God's great gifts.

Unfortunately, I soon became the child in the story. In my twenties, the sun began making me sick. I would become dizzy or nauseous, get a headache, and sometimes break into hives. I hated that I had to begin restricting my time in the sun. It got so bad that I could no longer even take a short walk in the sun without feeling sick. I didn't know why until my thirties, when I was diagnosed with lupus. Many people aren't aware that 80 percent of people with systemic lupus erythematous have hypersensitivity to the sun. Sun exposure in lupus patients has even recently been tied directly to kidney damage. Oh, how I long for the freedom of being outside in the sunshine!

As humans, we generally crave sunshine, as we can see by the research done on Seasonal Affective Disorder (SAD). When people aren't able to enjoy sunshine for an extended period, they tend toward depression. Just yesterday, when it was raining on the heels of two weeks of snow and ice, my husband remarked, "Can I just get a little sunshine, please?" In addition to our mood, we know the importance of vitamin D to our physical health and how it relates to sun exposure. Do you personally crave the warmth and freedom of the sun?

After a year of quarantine and social restrictions in 2020, I was yearning for some freedom. I wanted to get outside and go somewhere! When I could actually get on an airplane and take a vacation again, it felt like fantastic freedom. These may not be the kinds of freedoms Ephesians is specifically talking about, but I know God calls us to live an abundantly free life in Christ. I think this means God wants us to feel free to explore, free to expand, free to enjoy God's gifts—all of that. Most importantly, however, because of Christ, we are free of the burden of our sins and guilt, whether these sins were yesterday or thirty years ago. Thus, we are free in the Son; the Son of God has set us free from our burdens, and no disease or pandemic can take that ultimate gift away from us. So this week I challenge you to live abundantly free in the Son, as well as in the sun (if you are able).

Lord God, you offer us such wonderful gifts in this life, yet we burden ourselves and choose to live restricted lives. Help us to grasp and fully accept the ultimate gift of your Son, Jesus Christ, and begin to live abundantly free in him. We love you. Amen.

42. Prayer: Variable, Unceasing, Consistent

Be cheerful no matter what; pray all the time; thank God no matter what happens. This is the way God wants you who belong to Christ Jesus to live. —1 Thessalonians 5:16-18 (MSG)

This week, I can't get my mind off prayer. Recently, I've heard incredibly personal stories of the power of prayer and how it has changed individual lives. I've experienced that power in my own life, with others "holding me up" with their prayers when I felt like dropping into nothingness. I've experienced that while going through divorce and separation from my child (due to visitation). I've experienced that with chronic illness and chronic pain and the feeling that I just can't go on another day . . . yet I wake up and I do go on. Have you experienced this power? Have you participated in this power on behalf of others?

As Christians, I think we're called to this type of intercessory prayer (interceding for others; praying fervently for the needs of others). I think we're also called to other types of prayer. We need to talk with God about what we are feeling and what we think we need. We also need to be quiet, spending time alone with God. We need to try to listen to God's quiet voice in our lives. It's impossible to listen if we don't stop and pay attention. We have to discipline ourselves to make time in our lives for all types of prayer. I recommend that you also practice contemplative prayer—simply being with God. A good friend introduced me to this powerful practice that takes prayer to another level entirely.

I first started thinking about "praying without ceasing" (1 Thess 5:16 ESV) when Stephen Curtis Chapman released a song titled "Let Us Pray" in 1996. It is about praying all the time, all day long. I remember driving in my car, listening to this song, and beginning to pray. Prior to this, I had designated "prayer times," but since then, I have attempted to pray throughout the day. Some people call these "whisper prayers." They are tiny prayers muttered (or said silently) all day long, whenever you think of something.

I have attempted to teach my children this practice, since I wasn't introduced to it as a child. I do this out loud sometimes to remind them. I might say, "Thank you, God, for this beautiful blue sky," or "Please be with the paramedics in that ambulance and the people they are helping." It's nothing particularly deep or wise. It's just a simple, short prayer. It keeps me connected and grounded.

If prayer is not a part of your life, I encourage you to begin praying in whatever way you are comfortable. I promise that it's powerful. It can change your life . . . and the lives of others. It's as simple as talking to God about whatever you want to talk about. If you need prayer today, if you're at that point with your illness (or anything else) where you feel you have no more strength, I would be honored to pray for you. Please reach out to someone.

Lord God, there are so many ways we can interact with you through prayer. Thank you for this variability. I think you love all the ways we attempt to connect with you. Help us to make prayer a consistent priority throughout the day. Help us to stop now; be with you; talk with you. Please comfort all those who are hurting and don't feel the strength to pray. Forgive us when we rush by them with less important things. Thank you so much for this gift of prayer. Amen.

43. Everything's Falling Apart

By your words I can see where I'm going: they throw a beam of light on my dark path. I've committed myself and I'll never turn back from living by your righteous order. Everything's falling apart on me, GOD; put me together again with your Word. —Psalm 119:105-106 (MSG)

Is everything falling apart on you? Maybe you are watching your health slide downhill. Perhaps your disease is worsening. It could be that the number of arthritic joints you have is growing. Your chronic pain might be increasing. You may feel sicker and weaker by the day. You may honestly feel like your world is falling apart, but I would encourage you today to look to the word of God.

• Look to the word for "prayer power" when you feel weak. You can pray the Psalms. You can pray the Lord's Prayer, or you can find another Bible verse to pray. For example, reading the words "God is strong, and he wants you strong" (Eph 6:10) encourages me to pray for strength to do my work each day.

• Look to the word for validation that you are precious and valuable and loved. (See John 3:16; John 14:21; John 15:9; Romans 8:37.) Ephesians 5:1-2 is one of my favorites: "Mostly what God does is love you. Keep company with him and learn a life of love. Observe how Christ loved us. His love was not cautious but extravagant. He didn't love in order to get something from us but to give everything of himself to us. Love like that." This verse not only reminds us of God's extravagant love but also teaches us how to love others. You can do something valuable today. You can love God and others, no matter how bad you feel.

• Look to the word for courage and strength as well as for validation that God is always with you. For example, Isaiah 41:10 says, "Don't panic. I'm with you. There's no need to fear for I'm your God. I'll give you strength. I'll help you. I'll hold you steady, keep a firm grip on you." Isn't that great? God's got this, and God's got you. You are never alone. God is with you in your sickness and pain.

People like us, who are chronically ill, sometimes get stuck in thinking only about their health struggles. Yes, your health is important, and you should keep seeking to improve it. However, your health is not everything. It's not even the most important thing to seek. Seek Jesus. Seek the word of God in whatever way works for you today.

Dear Lord, help me to the look to your word as I struggle with my illness. Help me to focus on Jesus rather than the pain. Remind me of your love. Give me courage and strength for today. Help me realize that my life may not be ideal, but it is valuable, and I can still do good work through you. Amen.

44. Do Your Own Research

God wants us to use our intelligence, to seek to understand as well as we can. —1 Corinthians 12:2 (MSG)

I had another rough week with chronic illness: nausea; exhaustion; arthritis pain; insomnia; stomach cramps. I could go on, but I know you've heard more than enough. However, I want you to know that I'm not ready to give up and be a victim to these autoimmune diseases. I hope you're not ready to give up, either, because we're called to more than that. We're called to use our intelligence.

I'll admit that when I first got sick, I believed the "experts" who said I had to take this pill with its many side effects and that, even then, I would suffer forever. I went from specialist to specialist, all of them adding their preferred medications to my daily regimen. Sometimes this would make a symptom or two better, but often the meds would cause further complications. My list of medications grew and grew while I got sicker. I'm not saying doctors and medications are all bad. I'm almost certain they have saved my life three or four times in the last twenty years. For that, I am very grateful.

What I have learned, though, is not to take the advice of any expert without using my own intellectual resources. I constantly seek information. If my doctor suggests a new drug, I take the time to research it thoroughly. If I get an abnormal blood test, I immediately find out the implications and treatments. I keep my mind open to "alternative" treatments. I read every nutrition book that comes out. I listen to every lecture I can find on my many diagnoses and symptoms. As a result, despite my bad week, I am overall healthier than

I have been in years and on fewer medications. Regardless of what I was initially told, I've learned that some of my health is, in fact, under my control with the help of nutrition, movement, and other life choices. Although my genetics are not great, I can improve my health and my life quality. The fact that I can do *something* makes all the difference. It adds a sparkle of hope to my illness.

So many chronically ill people feel like their lives are out of control, but remember that God calls you to use your intelligence in all situations. To do this, I encourage you to read books and articles; listen to reputable scientists and providers; do your own research; study the body; and attempt to understand what is going on with your own health. I want you to know that there is hope for a better life. A few years ago, I would not have believed that I could feel better by improving my nutrition and eliminating seven medications. Reducing medications may not be an option for you (and it's something you must *not* do without consulting your doctor), but if you put your mind to it, I'm sure there's something you can do to improve your health. A little improvement makes a daily difference.

The reason I wrote this book is to attempt to provide hope for those with chronic illness. While our ultimate hope and help is Jesus Christ, sometimes you can provide a bit of your own hope if you work at it. God blessed us all with intelligence, so I think we should use it to the best of our abilities. Sometimes this intelligence helps us understand God better. Sometimes it helps us do our jobs better or helps us become better parents. Sometimes, however, it might just make us a bit healthier. It won't hurt to give it a try.

Dear Lord, thank you for giving us intelligence and resources. Help us do what we can to feel better and live better lives. Amen.

45. Hear My Prayer

Answer me when I call to you, my righteous God. Give me relief from my distress; have mercy on me and hear my prayer. —Psalm 4:1 (NIV)

My grandmother I called Mamma (pronounced Ma-maw) loved to tell the story of a conversation we had when I was five years old. I was worried about something, and she told me to pray about it. I told my grandmother that I had tried prayer and it didn't work. Being curious, she asked what I had prayed about. Apparently, I had prayed that my brother and I would switch birthdays. I waited a year, and God didn't switch them! So at that point, I was done with prayer. I don't remember this conversation at all, but I believe that it happened. I distinctly remember that I thought it was torture each year watching my brother celebrate his birthday and then having to wait *two extra days* to celebrate mine! Two days is a long time when you're that young, as I'm sure you'll remember.

Obviously, praying to switch your own birthday is a ridiculous request, but have you ever thought that you were "done" with prayer? You had prayed something diligently, with such strong belief, and yet nothing happened. You prayed for a better marriage. You prayed for another job opportunity. You prayed for healing from your chronic illness. Crickets. Nothing. So what are we to do? Give up and be done with prayer?

I prayed for a better marriage for fifteen years. That prayer was never answered in the way that I thought it would be. However, God answered it in a way I could never imagine in my wildest dreams when I was that young, suffering wife. Following divorce and remarriage,

I now have a very different, yet kind and supportive husband, along with a good and stress-free marriage.

I've prayed for healing now for so many years. Am I healed? No, but I'm a little better and I'm learning and growing. I also have a stronger faith. I know that God is with me each day as I'm dealing with these diseases. That is not the healing answer I was seeking, but it's an even more valuable answer.

I encourage you to keep praying no matter the outcome. Pray loudly and fervently if you want, crying out to God in your frustration. But pray with an open mind and heart. What if you don't get the "right" answer? What if, in fact, you get something far better?

Heavenly Father, we don't often understand your answers to our prayers. Thank you that you always hear us, and you go with us through each day, no matter what. Help us to keep asking and keep talking. Amen.

46. Fickle Cheer

And that's about it, friends. Be cheerful. Keep things in good repair. Keep your spirits up. Think in harmony. Be agreeable. Do all that, and the God of love and peace will be with you for sure. Greet one another with a holy embrace. All the brothers and sisters here say hello. —2 Corinthians 13:11-13 (MSG)

Do you find it hard to "be cheerful" and "keep your spirits up" while dealing with chronic illness? Surely you do. I do. So many people with chronic illness experience depression. While, fortunately, I don't deal with significant depression on a regular basis, the being cheerful is a stretch most days. It's hard to be cheerful when your head is splitting or your knee won't bend or you feel like throwing up. Can you relate? Sometimes your symptoms may get better and your cheerfulness meter may rise, but then it always seems to get knocked back down the next day.

The last two months, for example, I have been more cheerful and in better spirits, as my arthritis pain and stiffness have decreased significantly. This was due to a new medication I was injecting daily. I wasn't thrilled with the bruises all over my stomach, but it was worth the benefit. Two days ago, I got word from my doctor that this medication will no longer be available after this week. Wait, what? This medication has helped my arthritis more than anything in ten years. I was better and feeling more hopeful about a better quality of life. Now what will I do? Just like that, I can almost hear my happiness level plummeting. Honestly, I am not proud to confess that the decline in my spirits was so quick. It's not like I physically feel worse yet, since I'm currently still taking the medication. The anticipation of feeling worse, however, has erased my cheer.

This makes me feel fickle and disappointed in myself. I think I shouldn't let things like this get to me so much. For one thing, what I'm doing is basically worrying that I'm about to get worse again. I'm well aware that the Bible instructs me not to worry. The bigger reason I'm disappointed in myself, however, is that my cheer and my spirits, my ultimate joy, is in Jesus Christ. *He* is the reason that I can continue each day, fighting these diseases. *He* is the one who brings joy, no matter the circumstances. Why, then, do I continue to let these temporary, worldly symptoms dictate my moods? I should be further along in my journey toward Christ, such that my spirits aren't this variable. What is wrong with me?

Dear Lord, I confess my fickleness and my horrible habit of worrying. Please help me to rest in your love. I know you are with me no matter how I feel, and I thank you for that. Help me to cling to you and to somehow convey the joy of Jesus to others, whether I feel well or not. Amen.

47. Pay Close Attention

Pay close attention, friend, to what your father tells you; never forget what you learned at your mother's knee. Wear their counsel like a winning crown, like rings on your fingers.
—Proverbs 1:8-9 (MSG)

I've often thought about what my parents taught me, but I've never thought before about how what they taught me affects my chronic illness or, rather, my ability to deal with my chronic illness. The opposite messages I often received from them are both important in my fight against diseases like lupus.

Here's what I mean. The main message from my father was, "Work hard and don't be lazy." He works practically nonstop with rigorous discipline. He taunts his grandchildren (just like he did his children) with serenades of the old song "Lazy Bones" in order to wake them up. He doesn't believe in sleeping in, even on weekends. Fortunately, my dad does not have any chronic illnesses.

My mother, on the other hand, always nudges the messages of "Get extra rest and don't push yourself." In school, while Dad was pushing me to reach for a higher A, Mom was telling me to relax and not worry about my grade, as a B would be fine. Just this week, out of the blue, she texted me that I needed to rest more.

As I look back on my many years of disease, I can see that the two contradictory messages have both been important in my life. My father's message is important in fighting these diseases. It pushes me with a "work hard" message to learn all I can about nutrition and lifestyle factors and to be my own health advocate. It then enables me (with the discipline I developed as a child) to stick to a restricted diet and to give myself shots daily; to exercise when I don't want to move; and to research treatments—all while hoping and seeking a better quality of life.

My mother's message is highly important, also, particularly with lupus. Lupus is an unpredictable disease, better on some days and much worse on others. The constant symptom, however, is fatigue. It's always there—just at different levels. On the extremely exhausted days, when it's a big effort to shower, I've learned that I must go with Mom's message and get some extra rest. If I try to push through, I'll be paying for days. Giving yourself permission to rest is incredibly important with lupus.

Contradictory messages, then, can both be beneficial. You just have to know when to use which piece of wisdom. It occurred to me that maybe wisdom from our Godly parent is like that at times. Occasionally, when we read the Bible it can be confusing, and we think we're getting contradictory messages. What if, instead of either/or, it's both/and, and we just have to learn *when* to use which message? Some argue, for example, over whether it's your faith or your works that is most valuable to God (see James 2). I suspect it's both, and at certain times one must take precedence over the other. I try to learn all I can from many sources: the Bible; my parents; friends; books; movies; etc. There's so much wisdom to be found in contradictory (and controversial) opinions.

Lord, thank you for all the wisdom found in your word. Thank you also for the wisdom you give us through others. Help us to carefully sort through our stash of knowledge and to pull out just what is needed today, right now, in order to live our best. Amen.

48. Figuring It All Out

Trust God from the bottom of your heart: don't try to figure out everything on your own. Listen for God's voice in everything you do, everywhere you go; he's the one who will keep you on track. Don't assume that you know it all. Run to God!
—Proverbs 3:5-7

I've had a stressful week. How about you? My migraines were frequent and my arthritis pain was worse. The best treatment I had was discontinued. I have expensive medical testing coming up. My daughter dropped and broke her school-issued computer. I have some close family members and friends with new, life-threatening health challenges. My husband had the stomach virus all week, and he's supposed to be *the healthy one* in our family!

The most stressful situation for me right now, though, relates to personal decisions I am wrestling with. Not knowing which way to go or how to handle things, I was worrying and not sleeping. That's when I sat down for my daily Bible reading and read Proverbs 3:5-7. I really needed that. I let the words wash over me as I repeated them. I physically exhaled and felt my shoulders relax. What a relief. I had forgotten that it's not all on my shoulders. I don't have to figure out these life complications by myself.

What's *your* weekly list of stressful things? I know you're facing hard things, probably much harder than my load. I hope you will let these verses soak into your soul today. You don't have to figure it all out. You don't have to solve it. Rest—really rest—in the fact that you're not expected to. Take a few deep, slow breaths and just rest in God. Spend time with God. The more stressed you are, the more focused time you need alone with God. Just sit and listen and be. It doesn't seem like it right now, but God's got this.

Please take care of yourself the best you can this week. Remember to encourage and pray for others. Do what you can, and then trust God with the rest.

Dear God, I often get overwhelmed trying to figure everything out, and then you remind me, yet again, that I don't have to. Thank you for this reminder. Please help me to trust you and rest in you each day. Please guide me with your love. In the name of Jesus, Amen.

49. Day One or Day Two

Summing it all up, friends, I'd say you'll do best by filling your minds and meditating on things true, noble, reputable, authentic, compelling, gracious—the best, not the worst; the beautiful, not the ugly; things to praise, not things to curse. Put into practice what you learned from me, what you heard and saw and realized. Do that, and God, who makes everything work together, will work you into his most excellent harmonies. —Philippians 4:18 (MSG)

Do you ever think about what you think about? Listen to how you're talking to yourself today. Is your silent head voice "talking trash" or uplifting you? I'm becoming more aware the last couple of years of what I say inside my head and how that relates to how I feel, both emotionally and physically. What am I saying about me and about others? What am I saying silently about the world?

Do an experiment. Spend one day watching lots of horrible news and dwelling on everything that's wrong with the world. Throw in complaints about everyone around you, and then assess yourself and point out—*again*—all your own faults. How do you feel?

Spend day two *not* watching bad news (or violent TV) and forcing yourself to say good things about yourself and others. Remind yourself that God is in control of the world. Listen to some uplifting music; do some yoga; and, most importantly, read the word of God. Now how do you feel?

The Bible says to think and meditate only on certain types of things. It also says not to worry. Yet we often waste our thinking time with negativity. Why do we do this to ourselves? Who is making you do this? You are. It's under your control. You just have to bring it to your own attention, pray and ask for help, and work to change your thought patterns.

This can make a difference in your chronic illness as well. Yes, you *will* feel better if you spend your day like day two (instead of day one). Remember that the mind-body connection is always present. In addition, you can change how you think about your illness and your symptoms. Yes, you hurt, but is something just a smidge better than yesterday? Maybe your back still hurts, but your knee feels a bit better. Maybe your fingers and toes are tingling and uncomfortable (peripheral neuropathy), but you're not as nauseous as you were two days ago. Celebrate the tiny improvements rather than dwelling on the remaining pain. Give thanks for every small thing.

Here's an extreme example. Last night, I chopped off the side end of my right index finger while slicing cabbage for dinner. My finger is literally crooked right now because a substantial piece is missing! Before heading to urgent care (to get help to stop the bleeding), I told my daughters that at least my throbbing finger took my mind completely off my chronic back pain!

Lord God, help us to choose wisely what we spend time thinking about. Help us to become aware of what we are choosing to dwell on. Help us to think about good, uplifting, positive things, as your word says to do. Fill our hearts with praises rather than complaints. Help us to give thanks for the small improvements in our health. Amen.

50. Healing through Wisdom

Some people make cutting remarks, but the words of the wise bring healing. —Proverbs 12:18 (NLT)

I'm slowly working my way through the book of Proverbs, trying to savor the wisdom it brings. There's a lot to unpack. This week, Proverbs 12:18 resonated with me. As a chronic illness sufferer, any mention of "healing" perks up my ears (or thoughts). Don't we all want healing in the most desperate way, whether physical, emotional, or spiritual? How about all three?

I began thinking about where I try to find wisdom. I think we have to intentionally seek wisdom in our lives. The first place to look for wisdom is the Bible. The Bible says that if we ask God for wisdom, God will provide. Have you had the experience of reading the Bible, praying over it, and discovering something new, something that suddenly makes life better and different? It's a healing experience.

Where else do we search for wisdom? I search constantly in books that I read. Recently, I have found extraordinary wisdom in the writings of Richard Rohr, Eugene Peterson, and Pierre Teilhard de Chardin. In the past, I also found incredible wisdom in the writings of C. S. Lewis, Dietrich Bonhoeffer, and Barbara Brown Taylor. Wisdom can also lurk in novels, songs, and poems. Sometimes it pops up where you least expect it, like in a movie or TV show. I have found that something I read or watch or listen to can remind me of what is truly important. Sometimes it serves to center me. Often, I am convicted on how I spend my time or how I choose my own words. Other times, I'm reminded that this pain is fleeting or that suffering will serve a purpose.

The Message translation of this verse is "Rash language cuts and maims, but there is healing in the words of the wise." Do you hang around wise people? Wise people in my life have included my parents and grandparents, some teachers, and several close friends. Everyone has the experience of being around someone who is negative and critical versus another person who is wise, uplifting, and encouraging. I am blessed to have a few friends who I know will always tell me the truth and will also give me great, sincere advice when asked.

What about you? I hope you have some reliable wisdom-givers around you, but are *you* wise? Do you dish out "rash language" or harsh sarcasm that "cuts and maims" others, or are you giving out healing, wise words? In order to become better at sharing wisdom, we have to work at it day by day. As we seek wisdom, let's carefully choose healing words. Your words may make a difference for someone today on their healing journey.

Dear Lord, thank you for the many sources of wisdom you provide, in addition to the true wisdom of your word. We long to be wise, God. Lead us to use what little wisdom we possess to speak healing words to others. Amen.

51. Honoring Mom

Charm can mislead and beauty soon fades. The woman to be admired and praised is the woman who lives in the Fear-of-God. —Proverbs 31:30 (MSG)

I was studying the Proverbs 31 woman this week and considering all the character traits that I find in Proverbs 31:10-31. These jumped out at me: trustworthy, resourceful, generous, kind, hard-working, smart, purposeful, giving, skilled, quick to help others, organized, creative, positive, efficient, wise, praiseworthy, respectful of God. There's a lot to unpack in these verses. I don't know about you, but they give me a lot to work on.

Since, as I write, Mother's Day is Sunday, I considered these verses in reference to both my mom and my own mothering qualities. First, you should know that I hit the jackpot in the mom department. I was beyond blessed with the best mother in the world, one who always puts God and family first. She is the most generous person I know, always thinking of others. She is definitely a Proverbs 31 woman who frequently displays lots of the above qualities, but she really shines with generosity, kindness, and respect for God. In addition, I was further blessed with two wonderful Christian grandmothers, both of whom I had the opportunity to know well. So, fortunately, I had no shortage of good examples in my childhood.

Next, I considered what I specifically need to work on at this time in my life. First, I immediately released myself from the jumbled guilt-and-failure feelings evoked by the verses on sewing. Sewing is *not* my thing. That's okay. I have other skills. The Proverbs 31 woman is an example from another time and culture. Let the details go, I say, and focus instead on the character traits. Now that we've got that out of the way, it's time to pray and meditate on what we can work on right now in our own lives.

Being positive is a quality that needs some work in my life. After staying home for a year due to the pandemic, I'll admit that I had a hard time being positive every day. At times I've felt guilty about not being positive. Yes, I have several chronic illnesses that I have to deal with every day, but there is so much suffering in the world that it feels like I have no room to complain about my life. Once again, I need to remind myself to count my blessings and show more gratitude.

The second trait that I don't really need to work on but that sits uncomfortably with me is "hard-working." I am hard-working by nature, but sometimes my autoimmune diseases do not agree with work. I have days with so much fatigue and pain that working hard is not an option. Perhaps you've let yourself experience guilt over this, too, when it is completely out of your control. You must take care of your body. You must rest on the worst days. I'm telling you—and me—to *let it go*. You are hard-working when it's possible. That's enough. Maybe on the days when you are sick and can't work hard, you can work instead on being kind, as it's hard to remain kind and not cranky when you are hurting.

The bottom line is that we all have something or, more likely, many things to work on. I know I do. Sometimes we sludge through the day, however, and don't really consider what we're doing or what character traits we're displaying. Praying over a passage of Scripture like this can help us focus. Remembering that we're not alone in this transformation is the key. Yes, you and I are a work in progress. Let's ask God for help and continue to move forward toward the person we need to become.

My Lord and my God, your word reveals lots of character traits for me to work on. I want to change. I want to become better, but I need your help desperately. Help me every day. In the name of Jesus, Amen.

52. Pain Levels

Instead, you must worship Christ as Lord of your life. And if someone asks about your hope as a believer, always be ready to explain it. —1 Peter 3:15 (NLT)

My daily pain level has increased lately from about 2 to 6. This is a direct result of the fact that I can't get my medicine anymore. I was feeling sorry for myself yesterday, thinking maybe it would be better if I hadn't had a taste of the less painful life. Then, I wouldn't know what I was missing. If you're a chronic illness patient with daily pain, you likely know what I mean. Maybe they didn't stop production on a medicine that worked for you, but your medicine just stopped working. This is a common experience in people with arthritis. Medications work for a while, but then they don't, and you're left wondering if this increased pain level is your new normal. Other times, people have to stop medications because the side effects are too severe or dangerous. Either way, it is a disappointment to begin to experience relief and then have it snatched away.

I was talking with God about this and reminded that my hope is not in pain relief or a certain medication. Of course, I want to feel better, but my true hope is in Christ, whether I feel good or rotten. Although I don't understand sickness and suffering, I do trust in God. Also, as I've mentioned before in this book, I know that all this pain is temporary. So I will endure and remind myself of my blessings. Not only that, but I will seek joy around me. A good place to start, for me, is always nature and creation.

For example, yesterday my young daughter found a tiny baby bunny on our front sidewalk. Twenty minutes later, she found another one about four feet away on the lawn. After doing some research to see what I was looking for, I searched my yard for a rabbit's nest. I found it in my front flowerbed, right in front of our porch, hiding in plain sight under a bush and some ivy. There was a little pile of twigs and fur, with a burrow underneath. As I carefully placed the bunnies back in the nest, I was reminded once again of the delicate beauty and importance of all creatures. I said a silent prayer for their safety. This unexpected experience added a touch of joy to an otherwise difficult morning.

My Lord and my God, thank you for daily joys and blessings. Sometimes you provide simple joys right in front of me, if I will only agree to pause and look. Thank you that my hope is forever in you rather than in treatments or cures. Please continue to provide me with enough strength for each day. Amen.

53. The Voice of Many Waters

And I heard a sound from heaven like the roar of mighty ocean waves. —Revelation 14:2 (NLT)

And his feet like unto fine brass, as if they burned in a furnace; and his voice as the sound of many waters. —Revelation 1:15 (KJV)

Through Bible study recently, it came to my attention that the voice of Jesus is like the sound "of many waters" (see also Ezek 43:2 ESV). This hit my soul like a force, and deep inside me there was a resounding "YES!" I have always been drawn to water, even as a very young child. My favorite is the ocean, as you would know if you could see the pictures displayed in my home. Psalm 29:3 (NLT) says, "The voice of the LORD echoes above the sea."

With no ocean in sight, however, I will seek out a lake, river, stream, or even the little creek in my neighborhood. Honestly, the backyard fountains or swimming pool waterfalls of my friends will do in a pinch. If truth be told, I even like the sound of the faucet running, although I refrain from doing this excessively (out of respect for the environment).

Do you share my love of water sounds? It is the most peaceful sound I know. It calms me, calls to me, draws me close to God. I feel consistently closer to God at the ocean than I do anywhere else. So it makes sense to me that Jesus would sound like that. The voice of water, the voice of Jesus, resonates deeply in my soul as it soothes and heals.

I may be chronically ill, but I feel a little better at the beach. We could talk here about the electromagnetic qualities of the earth (as in grounding) and how they affect humans. Alternatively, we could talk about how the mind affects the body or how the spiritual nature affects the physical nature. There are a lot of theories about why people are drawn to oceans or to nature in general. However it works, I just know I feel better. It's not that I'm never sick when I go on a beach vacation, but I am overall a little better, a little more "okay," and maybe even a little more at peace with the fact that I am ill.

If you are overwhelmed today with pain, with nausea, or with the deep exhaustion that comes from pain-related insomnia, you might try seeking some flowing water. When you reach it, be still and quiet, breathe deeply, close your eyes, and listen to the voice of Jesus.

Thank you, Lord, for the gift of flowing water. Thank you for your forever flowing love. We are seeking your peace, calm, and love. Help us to stop and receive it. Amen.

54. Unfounded Guilt

Share each other's burdens, and in this way obey the law of Christ. —Galatians 6:2 (NLT)

Riding in the backseat on the way to yet another doctor's appointment for her mother (me), my nine-year-old daughter said, "I gotta hand it to you, Mom. I never thought you'd live this long!" After taking a minute to get over the shock of that statement, I told her that I work hard to be as healthy as possible and stick around. After reflecting on this for about a week, I've had many thoughts.

First, how sad that she has to grow up with a sick mom. How much time has she spent worrying about me? Does she think about my death a lot? Oh, the guilt that I have placed this burden on her young life!

Yet then I realize the alternative. I knew I was sick with lupus when I chose to have her. I knew the risks to her and to me. Yes, she was premature as a result, but look at her: a beautiful, happy, energetic child! Having her was obviously, without a doubt, the right choice.

What do *you* do with your guilt over being sick? Do you worry that you are a burden to your children, spouse, parents, or friends? How much time and energy do you waste on this destructive thought process?

Galatians 6:2 says, "Share each other's burdens, and in this way obey the law of Christ." So maybe others help you carry the burden of your illness. That's okay—you didn't choose this life of chronic illness, but here it is, and you need help carrying it. The people around you have other types of burdens (psychological, physical, spiritual, financial, etc.). Pay attention and notice them. What can you help carry?

And get rid of that unfounded guilt. This sharing of burdens is what Jesus commanded.

Here's another verse that might also help: "Don't let your hearts be troubled. Trust in God, and trust also in me" (John 14:1 NLT).

Heavenly Father, we hate placing burdens on others, but that's part of it, isn't it? Help us to accept this and, in turn, notice and carry the burdens of others, just as you intended. Amen.

55. How Deep and Healing

And may you have the power to understand, as all God's people should, how wide, how long, how high, and how deep his love is. May you experience the love of Christ, though it is too great to understand fully. —Ephesians 3:18-19 (NLT)

It's Father's Day as I write this. I am so blessed to have a wonderful father who is still with me. I also was fortunate to have two incredible grandfathers in my life as a child. As a bonus, I now have a kind father-in-law, although that was not always the case.

Not all are so lucky in the father department, I know. Many people have absent fathers, uninvolved fathers, or worse, abusive fathers. Twenty years ago, I had a terrifying father-in-law. He kicked his wife, shoved his daughter, and showered them with hateful comments about their unworthiness. Nothing he said was up for discussion, as he ruled like a tyrant in that house. He once pointed a gun at me and told me to get my then-blanking-husband out of his house or he would blow our heads off. Nice guy.

I'm well aware that many people in this world are only exposed to *that* type of father. I wonder how difficult, then, it is for them to be able to grasp the love of our heavenly Father? Did you know that people who have experienced more adverse childhood events, like abuse from fathers, are much more likely to be chronically ill later in life? If this is part of your story, then I pray that you had a mother or a grandmother or someone, anyone, in your life who showed you genuine, compassionate love. Please know that God's love goes beyond all human love. It is unconditional and eternal, and nothing and no one can take it from you. Romans 8:38a states, "And I am convinced that nothing can ever separate us from God's love." If you run to your heavenly Father, he will never, ever hurt you. God will only love you deeply, and God's love is healing—the kind of medicine that goes beyond autoimmune disease and soaks into your very soul.

Heavenly Father, may we cast off any negative effects of the men in our past. You are not like that. You are good and loving, always and forever. Please heal our hearts and souls with your love. Amen.

56. Exhaustion

My health may fail, and my spirit may grow weak, but God remains the strength of my heart; he is mine forever.
—Psalm 73: 26 (NLT)

Recently, because of a new treatment, I am better. I have more energy than normal. I can do more things, and I don't have to rest all afternoon, as I used to. I am so thankful.

I am very aware, however, that many chronic illness patients are *not* doing well. They are suffering. They are exhausted and unable to function as they want to. Maybe that's you.

Last week, I had two friends with autoimmune diseases talk with me about their fatigue and sickness. One said she was so sick that she just didn't know what to do. The other friend said that when she wakes up, she is just as exhausted as when she went to bed. I completely understand what they are saying and where they are coming from, because I've been there. I have felt that way for years.

I hurt for them. At times, I even feel guilty that I feel better than they do right now. Recognizing quickly that such guilt is obviously a waste of time, I wondered what I could do to ease their burdens. I obviously can't take away their pain and fatigue, but how can I make it a bit more bearable? I can encourage them and try to spark hope and listen to them. They know when I listen that I truly understand what they're feeling, because they have watched me suffer, too.

That is what I can do with the more "healthy time" I've been given. I can try to help others who are less healthy. I can be there for others while it's possible for me to do this in a more active way. Most importantly, I can support them in prayer. I am reassured by the fact that these two friends both have a strong faith. Their soul-strength is solid. I know they will be okay since they are only struggling with physical strength. Physical health is fleeting and fickle. Failing health is difficult to manage and deal with, without a doubt, but if your strength is in God, you can sustain and maybe even grow through the pain.

If you're able today, encourage someone. Be there for them. If you're the one who is suffering, accept some help. Welcome prayers for strength. No matter who you are or how you're feeling, stop now and connect to God, who is the source of real, enduring strength.

Lord God, please strengthen those who are sick and exhausted today. Give them hope for better tomorrows. Bring a friend into their lives to encourage them. In Jesus's name, Amen.

57. God Has Seen Your Misery

Then the people of Israel were convinced that the LORD had sent Moses and Aaron. When they heard that the LORD was concerned about them and had seen their misery, they bowed down and worshiped. —Exodus 4:31 (NLT)

I've been listening to a good preacher talk about Exodus for a few weeks now. I must admit that when I first heard she was switching to the Old Testament, I wasn't altogether thrilled. I can read and think about Jesus all day long, but I really have to push myself to read through all the numbers and descendant lists and tabernacle details in the Old Testament. Once again, however, I was proven wrong, as there are some excellent lessons, stories, and verses that I had forgotten about. I am looking at Exodus with renewed interest now.

Exodus 4:31 speaks to a universal truth. Everyone wants to be loved. We want to know that we are not alone. We want to know that we are cared about. We want someone to see how much we are suffering. Even if people don't seem to notice or care at times, all these needs are fulfilled in our Creator God. "The LORD was concerned about them and had seen their misery." That is comforting on a deep level.

God sees your misery—how you suffer every day. God sees your pain and cares about you. You do not struggle with these diseases alone. You are loved all the time. Please sit still before God, and try to feel God's love. Dwell on this verse and pray about it. Then know, with a mind, heart, and soul kind of knowing, that the Lord is with you in this.

On your better days, when you are able, take this loving message to others so that they, too, may know they never suffer alone.

Lord God, we thank you that you love us so deeply and completely. Thank you for the promise that you see our misery and that you care. It helps to know this and to know that you walk through it all with us. When we are stronger, help us to share this message with others. Amen.

58. Fully Seeing Beauty

Be glad; rejoice forever in my creation! And look! I will create Jerusalem as a place of happiness. Her people will be a source of joy. —Isaiah 65:18 (NLT)

Riding in the car back to the resort after a helicopter tour of Kauai's waterfalls on our ten-year anniversary trip, I couldn't gaze at the scenery. I actually had to close my eyes to God's creation. I had absorbed so much incredible beauty on that helicopter, fully seeing all the waterfalls, mountains, ocean waves, valleys, rivers, greenery, and even rainbows, that I felt physically, emotionally, and spiritually too full. There was a heaviness in my chest. My heart was overwhelmed with the immensity of God's beauty, and I felt suddenly exhausted. I thought, "I need to sleep. I need to go to bed right now" (although it was only 4 pm). I couldn't stand to see any more of that beautiful island right then. That sounds crazy, doesn't it?

Thinking about the experience later, I thought that if this was a glimpse of what heaven will be like, or the new creation of heaven on earth, then how will I be able to take it? God is too beautiful—too good—and I think I am not yet strong enough to be more completely in God's presence. Am I too impure or too unholy (or un-wholely!)? Or is God too stunningly beautiful for me to see and absorb?

I'm reminded of Exodus 3:5: "Do not come any closer," the Lord warned. "Take off your sandals, for you are standing on holy ground." Was Moses too impure to be near God, or was God too good, or both? In my Hawaii experience, I felt like I was being told, "Shut your eyes, Julie, for you are seeing Holiness and Beauty, and you are not yet prepared."

What is strange is that even though I felt exhausted and overwhelmed by the Beauty, I craved the promise of more.

Thank you, Lord, for the glimpse of what is to come. May I be aware and open to more such glimpses in my everyday life. May we all fully see what you have created, and may we be able to translate these experiences into hope. Amen.

59. Joy Flickers

Whatever happens, my dear brothers and sisters, rejoice in the Lord. I never get tired of telling you these things, and I do it to safeguard your faith. —Philippians 3:1 (NLT)

Friday morning, I schlepped out to my back porch, my whole body aching from arthritis, feeling like I hadn't rested at all. I plopped down in a chair with my coffee. The coffee was weak and bitter, but I was too tired to go fix it. I insincerely thanked God for the day and began to pray. I prayed for family and friends who are sick with serious illnesses (cancer, stroke, lupus). I prayed for the fearful and desperate people of Afghanistan. I prayed for healing and provision for people in Haiti after a recent earthquake. I prayed for two family members in quarantine for Covid and for the whole virus situation that is ramping up yet again. I felt heavy and depressed.

This is no joke. I had just prayed, "Thy will be done on earth as it is in heaven," when I felt a presence. A hummingbird flew within two feet of me and hovered there for about ten seconds. I felt an instant flicker of joy and a slight lightening of the load. This had never happened before, as I don't have a hummingbird feeder (although I'm thinking I should get one). The hummingbird flew away, but I looked around and immediately saw a blue jay, a robin, a cardinal, and a sparrow all within twelve feet of me. Suddenly I felt like I was in a Disney movie. I laughed. The joy that seemed impossible two minutes earlier was suddenly there.

As I think about those bits of creation-joy, which often come to me in the form of animals, I realize that I receive them daily from my annoying cat who won't quit rubbing her face against mine and from my sweet fifteen-year-old dog who follows me everywhere. I also thought of a tiny squirrel I saw recently by a pool, standing on its hind legs to beg me for a corn chip. (Yes, of course, I fed it—repeatedly.) It can be hard to find joy in the world, with the pain of chronic illness, the suffering of those around us, and devastating world events. I can't really tell you how to find it today, except that prayer seems to be an avenue to get a joy flicker. Another key, I think, is quietly looking around you and noticing things. Concentrate on gentle, quiet things.

These joy flickers don't last, as we're bombarded soon with yet another problem, but we have to keep looking and seeking. We must be *sincerely* thankful that they are there.

Dear Lord, thank you so much for the flickers of joy you provide us amid all the pain and suffering. We need them, and we need you. Forgive us when we are insincere in our thankfulness. Forgive us when we miss so much around us, distracted by our own pain. Thank you that you have overcome all the heaviness. Thank you for the knowledge that you are in control, even when we cannot see it. Amen.

60. Deceptive Fire

Let no one deceive you with empty words, for because of such things God's wrath comes on those who are disobedient.
—Ephesians 5:6 (NIV)

In early 2007, I had a deceptive house fire. We lit a fire in the fireplace on the second floor. The room began to fill with smoke. The firefighters came and said there was no fire, and then they left. The fire in the fireplace was out, but the house got smokier. The second time the fire department was called, they brought a device that could "see" through the walls to detect a fire. Sure enough, it was burning behind the walls, out of sight. Everything looked fine on the outside, yet inside it was turmoil and destruction.

It turns out that the cause of the fire was also a form of deception. The previous owners, we were told by the firefighters, had caulked around the brick inside the fireplace instead of using refractory mortar that can withstand high heat. The caulk or silicone they used decomposed in the high temperatures, allowing the fire to seep into the walls behind the fireplace. It crawled down to the first floor and burned the front porch. Before we had moved in, someone had "fixed" that fireplace so that it looked great, but it wasn't what it seemed. It wasn't safe.

How have you been burned by deception? Was it a medication that promised to make your life better, but its side effects were more destructive than the original symptom? Was it the life-changing betrayal of a friend or spouse? Was it finding out that someone you thought was following Christ was really only focused on their own personal gain?

How about the "empty words" all around us in society today? Does it often seem that everyone is trying to deceive you, and you're not sure who you can actually believe anymore?

I think we need to be discerning in this world and not immediately accept what someone says or that what we see is, in fact, what is there. It took me a while to learn this, as I began this life embarrassingly naive and gullible. I suppose we all do, but I clung to that immature pattern too long. Hebrews 5:14 states, "But solid food is for the mature, for those who have their powers of discernment trained by constant practice to distinguish good from evil."

Some people never get there, or never try. This week, I watched someone my age read something on Facebook and run to others with it like it was verified truth. Really?

When I hear something significant now, I question it. I think about it and research it. I hold it up to the lens of Christ and my values. No, I don't always get it right, but I continue to try to find truth.

When my doctor suggests a new medication, I research it extensively. When I hear something on the news, I verify it with several other sources. When a preacher makes a novel statement, I search the Bible, pray, and think about the truth of that idea.

The other side of this is my own deception. Am I always careful to speak only the truth? Am I truthful with myself or with God? We know we can't trick God, so why do we try to put a positive spin on our choices?

Holy God, help us be discerning in this world. Forgive us when we are too eager to believe rampant lies. Forgive us also when our own deception is part of the problem. We are learning, yet we admit that we are painfully slow. Grant us wisdom. Amen.

61. Why Do You Want Us Broken?

That is why the LORD says, "Turn to me now, while there is time. Give me your hearts. Come with fasting, weeping, and mourning." —Joel 2:12 (NLT)

God, why do you request specifically that sad people come to you? Is it because they are the ones who are open or the ones broken apart? Do they have room for you to fill in the cracks of their lives?

Happy people are often busy people. Their lives are rolling along in a smooth routine.

Sad, pain-filled people suddenly have time. Their routines are interrupted by something they didn't anticipate and didn't want. They are having trouble functioning as normal, while discovering that whatever used to be "normal" might not have been so important after all. Not knowing what to do, they look around. They do a lot of sitting, with time slipping by.

How about fearful people? Can we group them with all the weeping and mourning people? In my experience, significant fear comes with weeping, so I'm going to say it qualifies.

My nine-year-old is currently sick with Covid symptoms. This is what I have feared for a year and a half. This is why I kept her out of school all last year, locked away from society. This fall, I sent her back, and she got sick three weeks in. You can bet I'm turning to God. Time stops, or drags, and nothing seems to matter besides my sick child.

Was there weeping involved? At the doctor's office, she repeatedly said, "Mama, I just want a hug." There were tears from both of us.

Touch is healing, yet I'm denying her that. Am I cruel and selfish? Or am I simply being careful as an autoimmune patient, one who has been told repeatedly that I must avoid Covid? I know that not having a mother would be much, much worse than a few days with no hugs, yet it hurts deeply to deny her.

Does God want us broken? That seems cruel, doesn't it? Yet mourning, weeping, fearing—they make us listen. These strong emotions force us to stop and be present. When a best friend dies (been there), time stops. When a child is really sick (there now), life stops. You can't work because you can't think, and you can't care about work the way you normally would. You can pray, though. Sometimes the prayers are a simple "help her" or "help me," but they're still prayers.

God, why do you want us to feel broken and helpless? Can't we give you our hearts another way? Even if we don't understand the reasons for this, help us to turn to you with our true hearts and our deepest feelings. We need to feel your presence and your comfort, Lord. Help us. Amen.

62. Fickle Joints

We also pray that you will be strengthened with all his glorious power so you will have all the endurance and patience you need. May you be filled with joy. —Colossians 1:11 (NLT)

People with arthritis need extra amounts of endurance and patience. What has always struck me as crazy about my arthritis is the way it moves around. I have two types of joint pain. First, I have joints that hurt every day and have hurt for years. Yes, I hate those joints, but at least I know what I'm getting each morning. I know they will hurt, and they do. I do the best I can to endure the pain.

Second, I have other fickle, unpredictable joints that may hurt like they're trying to kill me for a couple days, or even a couple of months, and then one day, with no warning, they ease up. Sweet, unexpected relief is there, but I remind myself not to get too comfortable because that excruciating pain will pounce on another unsuspecting joint very soon.

At times, I think I'm crazy. Wasn't the right knee killing me yesterday, and now I can walk up the stairs just fine? What in the world is wrong with me? I can't tell you how many times I've brought this up to my rheumatologist, this moving-around joint pain. Each time, he patiently confirms that it's normal. He can't explain why it happens, but it does.

Those "temporary" arthritic joints require a special kind of patience. When I get a new bad joint, I try to tell myself it's only temporary. I need to be patient and endure it. Work through the pain, but don't push it too much.

Enter my right hip. Two weeks ago, it started getting very sore. Uh-oh, I thought. This is a new area. I would wake up with it sore each morning, try to be patient, stretch it out, and go on with my day enduring dull pain. Okay, I can work through this, I thought. This week, the soreness didn't stretch out. It stayed *all* day. Then, a few days ago, I began having "episodes" in which the joint felt like it caught on something and just refused to work. When I forced it, there was major sharp pain.

Twice this week, I was stranded. I suddenly couldn't walk. Friday night, my husband and I went on an outside date, and we had walked a couple of blocks when, all of a sudden, my hip joint said no more. He had to leave me on the street corner downtown and go get the car.

The difficult thing about these "temporary," moving arthritic joints is that sometimes they become permanent. So now I'm enduring and trying to be patient. I'm hoping I get my hip back sometime soon.

Even if you have never experienced this weird type of pain, I know you have pain you must endure. You probably have both physical and emotional pain that calls for patient endurance. Sometimes it's temporary, like the flu. Sometimes it's permanent, like the death of a family member.

The temporary ones are easier, of course, except when they turn permanent, like a betrayal that turns into a divorce or an illness that turns into terminal cancer. We just never know, do we?

I have no easy answers for getting through all this. I just pray for God's strength, that God will fortify us so that we may endure this pain, whether for a day or for the rest of our lives. My experience tells me that God's strength is definitely permanent and never-ending. We can draw from that strength the patience and endurance we need for this day.

Lord God, thank you for your permanence. We ask that you give us enough strength for just this day, so that we may endure our pain. Amen.

63. Endless Prayers

Let me say first that I thank my God through Jesus Christ for all of you, because your faith in him is being talked about all over the world. God knows how often I pray for you. Day and night I bring you and your needs in prayer to God, whom I serve with all my heart by spreading the Good News about his Son. —Romans 1:8-9 (NLT)

I pray daily for the needs of others. Sometimes there are situations, however, that require me to pick up the pace so that I am praying frequently for a particular person. Maybe the prayer doesn't last long. For example, my teenager was gone all last night, spending the night with a friend. Every time I woke up (a lot), I said a little prayer for her safety. (Please don't tell her, because somehow I know that she would be very annoyed!)

When someone is ill, you often don't know the length of the sickness or how long that person will need fervent prayer. My father-in-law became really ill a week ago. He has been in the hospital for seven days in severe pain, and we are praying consistently for relief. We hope this is a temporary need, and we pray for healing.

For the last month, a good friend had asked me to pray for her friend, who has been in the hospital with Covid. I have done this and have checked with her every few days for updates. A couple weeks ago there was some improvement, but then her health declined again. She passed away last week. I felt this loss strongly, although I did not know the woman. I felt sad for my friend, of course, but even more so for the woman's children and husband.

In praying for her for a month, I spent some time thinking about what she must be going through. I imagine that her anguish in facing possible death had a lot to do with her children. When she passed, I wondered what happened to those feelings. Although I've been taught that there's no sadness after death, it is beyond my comprehension how this woman could no longer be sad about the grief of her young children. If I had been in her shoes, knowing I was dying, my most extreme worry would be about my children dealing with my death and then having to grow up without their mother. How do I know this?

I know because when my daughters were two and ten, I thought it was a possibility for me, and I thought about this scenario a lot. Probably everyone who has lupus has seriously considered their own death, knowing that they have a chronic illness that increases their mortality rate. At that particular point, however, my health was deteriorating, and I was having more and more issues with my nervous system. My neurologist made a comment that if I didn't get my lupus under control, then I might not be around in five years. Never has another sentence grabbed my attention so completely. I took that statement seriously, had a devastating conversation with my husband, and got to work writing a will. Then, I went to my rheumatologist, requested an intense new treatment, and, thankfully, things turned around for me. During that difficult time, however, I asked people to pray. That was hard for me to do, but I knew it was important, and I believed in it. I believe in it still.

Prayer is scriptural, and it's important. Jesus taught his disciples to pray the Lord's prayer. I think prayer is one of our main jobs as Christians, and I take it seriously. Sometimes people get better. Sometimes people arrive home safely. Sometimes, however, they don't. Why? I have absolutely no idea, but, no matter the outcome, I know the act of prayer in important, and I think that it is somehow lasting.

Some people say prayer changes the one praying rather than the one (or situation) being prayed for/about. I think it's actually both, but it's so much more than that. Prayer is a way for us to carry each other, and we are called to do this. Even beyond that, perhaps prayer has a deeper, higher meaning, something that we can't yet understand.

One excellent thing about prayer is that everyone can do it. You don't have to be physically fit to pray for someone. You don't have to get out of the house or even out of bed. Prayer is the perfect job for someone with chronic illness!

Who needs your endless prayers today?

Do you need to ask for some fervent prayers for yourself?

God, I don't understand prayer, but I know you call me to it, and I am thankful for that. Your word says that the Spirit will help me in my prayers. I could really use the help, so please guide and teach me daily. In Jesus's name, Amen.

64. Shot Mishap

Rejoice in our confident hope. Be patient in trouble, and keep on praying. —Romans 12:12 (NLT)

Be joyful in hope, patient in affliction, faithful in prayer. —Romans 12:12 (NIV)

Many of you know that mornings are tough for people with arthritis. You wake up feeling like the tin man in need of oil. (I heard that from someone else once, but I can't remember who. It's a great analogy for how I feel!) You shuffle around the best you can, gradually stretching your body until it slowly begins to function better.

Well, apparently, I hadn't done enough stretching on Friday morning. Every day, I give myself two shots for arthritis in my abdomen. When I shifted to inject my left side Friday, I pulled my back and shoulder on the right. So, in trying to help my general arthritis pain, I created a new intense pain! I just had to laugh. I knew immediately that this wasn't just a momentary pain. I spent the rest of the day lathering on pain cream and not moving much at all. It hurt even to turn my head.

It's still very sore today, but I've decided to get on with it. I had house cleaning to do, as well as some outside chores, and I got up and did them—pain or not. I am being "patient in affliction," but I'm also getting on with my life.

Affliction in this verse can be any kind of suffering or pain, small and large. It can be enduring chronic illness. It can be struggling through a divorce or a natural disaster. It can be facing a court trial or fleeing a dangerous country.

In all of these circumstances, where can we find joyful hope? Does it really come before patience? I think not; it only comes through prayer. It comes directly from Christ. So maybe this verse should start with prayer, which gives us hope and joy through a relationship with God. Then we are able to relax enough in that hope and joy so that we can be more patient through our afflictions. This enables us to continue on our journey.

It seems like a cycle to me. The best thing we can do is to keep the praying consistent. Rest in the confident hope we have through Jesus. Those afflictions will always come in some form or another, but God will be with us through them so that we can patiently endure.

I'm not always great at the patient part, so maybe I need more of the praying part. How about you?

Lord, we come to you in prayer. We ask for an abiding relationship with you. Thank you for your love, which brings us joy and hope. Please be with us in all types of afflictions, and give us the necessary patience to endure each one. In Jesus's name, Amen.

65. People to the Rescue

The righteous person faces many troubles, but the LORD comes to the rescue each time. Psalm 34:19 (NLT)

Sometimes the Lord comes to the rescue through people. My husband and I were having a rare, much-needed date night a couple of weeks ago. It's not often that both of our daughters are gone for the night. We were watching a movie at home after getting takeout. About halfway through, the next-door neighbor called. They were downtown and their car wouldn't start. Could someone come get them? Now, I must confess our first reaction was a groan, but helping them was the right thing to do, so we did it.

I've been on the other end of this. My brother has come to my rescue in the midst of car troubles at least a couple of times. There's a different kind of anxiety in being stranded alone on the road. It's comforting when you know that you can count on someone to come rescue you.

There are many kinds of rescue. The process of my divorce was long and draining. Each week brought another piece of bad news. Throughout all the mess, my friend Sheri was a big part of my rescue team. She spent time with me each week, in person, despite her busy schedule of family and career. She always told me, "It'll get better." I didn't believe it because I saw no evidence of it. She believed it for me. She refused to let me withdraw, and she refused to let me give up. That's a powerful rescue, and one I'm forever grateful for.

Chronic illness requires a lot of rescuers. Sometimes it's your doctor. Sometimes it's family or friends. It can be as simple as someone cooking a meal for you so you don't have to get up and do it or even think about it. A simple rescue can help you make it through a painful, fatigued day.

I encourage you to allow people to rescue you when you need it. And when you don't, look around and find someone else that you can rescue.

Heavenly Father, thank you for sending rescuers. Help us to lower our pride and accept help when we need it. May we be less self-centered and, when able, be ready to provide a simple rescue for someone else. Amen.

66. Waiting Quietly

Let all that I am wait quietly before God, for my hope is in him. He alone is my rock and my salvation, my fortress where I will not be shaken. —Psalm 62:5-6 (NLT)

Two of my close family members have been sick this past week. In fact, they were both in the ER at the exact same time (in different cities). Of course, having autoimmune diseases that increase my risk for bad outcomes with Covid and the flu, I could not be in the hospital with either one of them.

I'm sure many of you were also denied the opportunity to be with sick loved ones during the pandemic, whether because of your own chronic illnesses or because of the restrictions in place. It's hard to take, because your whole being tells you that you should be there. You feel helpless.

So you wait and you pray and you constantly call and text for updates on your loved one's condition. Since it's nearly impossible to wait patiently, you settle for waiting "quietly before God" with your hope in God. You lean on God as your rock, fearing that you may not be able to take what comes next but knowing that you are not alone in it.

Waiting and praying is really all you can do sometimes. It has to be enough. When the anxiety increases, the Bible can help: "Do not be anxious about anything, but in everything by prayer and supplication with thanksgiving let your request be made known to God. And the peace of God, which surpasses all understanding, will guard your hearts and your minds in Christ Jesus" (Phil 4:6-7 NIV).

I often have this cycle going: a little waiting, a lot of anxiety, time for prayer again, and then some peace, followed by more waiting.

Hint: It helps if you can cycle through this with someone else.

Dear God, we hate it when our loved ones are sick. We want to be with them and help in some tangible way. Take care of them for us. In the meantime, help us through our anxious cycles and lead us to more peace. Amen.

67. Belief, Faith, Hope

This is why we work hard and continue to struggle, for our hope is in the living God, who is Savior of all people and particularly of all believers. —1 Timothy 4:10 (NLT)

Thanks to a good friend and a book study she painstakingly organized, I've been thinking a lot lately about belief, faith, and hope. Some people use the terms "belief" and "faith" interchangeably, but I think there's a huge difference. The leap from belief in God to faith in God is a big one, and it takes time and the integration of life experience with your beliefs.

Faith is deeper than belief. You can believe in God and yet not have faith that God is ultimately in control and will set everything right. You can believe there is a God and yet not know God. You can believe but be unable to rest in the idea that "All shall be well, and all shall be well, and all manner of thing shall be well" (Julian of Norwich).

I know I have faith because I trust God. I know I have faith because I spend time with God daily. This is not only a discipline (although discipline is required), but it's a privilege, something I love to do. The discipline part is making myself stop, prioritize this, and do it regularly. Once I'm there, however, with a quieted heart and mind, I am home in a way that only God can create.

That "home" feeling and that ability to rest because "all shall be well" lead me to the blessed ability to hope. As 1 Timothy 4:10 says, "our hope is in the living God." As a result of this hope, we can "work hard and continue to struggle." We can get through the days because of this hope.

We must work hard at parenting, at our jobs, at volunteering, or at whatever our work entails. We must struggle with our problems, whether they are financial, familial, or medical. As people with chronic illness, we have the additional struggle of constantly dealing with symptoms while doing our work. Sometimes those symptoms even overtake us, such that we simply cannot complete our work that day. Still, as believers, we continue to have hope.

Are belief, faith, and hope consecutive, like you get done with belief and move on to faith and then to hope? It's much more complex than that. Remember the verse "Lord, I believe; help my unbelief" (Mark 9:24)? We continually move through cycles of belief, faith, and hope throughout our lives. Sometimes we even lose sight of hope when we let our struggles overwhelm us. I think most of us do not reach the levels of belief, faith, and hope that we need in this life.

Lord God, I seek greater faith and hope through you. Help me in my work, my struggles, my health. Help me integrate my life experiences, good and bad, into more growth toward you. Amen.

68. Dripping Mud

I don't mean to say that I have already achieved these things or that I have already reached perfection. But I press on to possess that perfection for which Christ Jesus first possessed me. No, dear brothers and sisters, I have not achieved it, but I focus on this one thing: Forgetting the past and looking forward to what lies ahead, I press on to reach the end of the race and receive the heavenly prize for which God, through Christ Jesus, is calling us. —Philippians 3:12-14 (NLT)

I don't know about you, but I have spent way too much time with my mind in the past. Parts of my mind were stuck in three areas:

• Things I could have done if I hadn't become ill
• Things I regret or decisions I regret making
• Trauma/abuse/bad memories that I couldn't stop thinking about

Some chronic illnesses are not permanent and some are, but by the definition of "chronic," the pain and sickness seem to go on forever. If a person is sick for any extended amount of time, I would imagine they would have regrets of things they would have liked to do that they couldn't do. Someone may have thoughts like, "If I hadn't been sick, I wouldn't have missed that graduation." I'll share with you some of my past regrets due to sickness. I wish I hadn't had to stop seeing patients. I wish I hadn't spent so much time in bed, missing family activities. I wish I could have hiked, kick-boxed, run, etc. I wish I could work outside of the home without worrying that I will catch something that will kill me (this was even before the pandemic). Do these types of thoughts help my joy and gratitude for today?

Then I have regrets about life choices. I wish I hadn't fill-in-the blank. Some of these are things I just want to kick myself for—lost opportunities or things I didn't try when I could have (before I was sick). Others are things I regret doing or life choices I made that I shouldn't have made. Some come with guilt, while others just have regret attached. Now we know that, through the grace and mercy of Jesus Christ, we are forgiven for our sins. We just have to confess, like David in Psalm 32:5, who said, "Finally, I confessed all my sins to you and stopped trying to hide my guilt. I said to myself, 'I will confess my rebellion to the LORD.' And you forgave me! All my guilt is gone." From that statement, it seems like this should be a quick, easy process, like you confess and the guilt is instantly gone. My experience is different. Guilt likes to hang on to me, and I must let it drip away like mud. It takes some scrubbing and repetition, and a trace of it tends to want to stick around as a reminder.

Although all three of the categories I listed above are joy-stealers, the third is the worst. If you are stuck reliving the negative parts of your past, then you are simply not living fully today. I don't believe God wants this type of life (or lack of life) for us. Some of my child-hood trauma/past abuse I dealt with in my twenties, but probably only because someone pointed out to me that it was a problem and I needed to work on it. Counseling was somewhat helpful at the time, but I had to commit to doing the work. My adult trauma had been shoved into a dark compartment of my mind, which leaked out in bad dreams and occasional flashbacks interrupting my day. Sometimes I would suddenly realize what I was reliving it and think, "Why am I wasting time thinking about this again?" Ignoring it wasn't working, so I had to address it. I finally made a conscious choice to pull it all to the surface, and I worked on this during the pandemic. It helped to have some extra time. It was painful but worth it. Nightmares are few now.

Oswald Chambers (2017) says, "Our yesterdays present irrep-arable things to us: it is true that we have lost opportunities which will never return, but God can transform this destructive anxiety into a constructive thoughtfulness for the future. Let the past sleep, but let it sleep on the bosom of Christ." I usually think about anxiety in light of worrying about things that might happen in the future. As I read this quote, I realized that dwelling on negative past memories and regrets also causes "destructive anxiety." However, I can choose to let God transform it all. Who needs extra anxiety when we have enough to deal with right now, today?

I hope you will join me in trying to move past the past and let go of all types of regrets. Let the sick-losses go; let the guilt go; and commit to working through the trauma. Let's learn what we can in the process and allow Christ to use our wounds and regrets to help us move forward through grace. Freedom and joy are at stake.

Heavenly Father, we don't want to be stuck in the past anymore. We want to live joyfully in you today and join fully in your work for a better future. Help us release the past and release ourselves from it. In Jesus's name, Amen.

69. Take a New Grip

So take a new grip with your tired hands and strengthen your weak knees. Mark out a straight path for your feet so that those who are weak and lame will not fall but become strong. —Hebrews 12:12 (NLT)

I haven't written for a couple of weeks because I had the flu. While I was thankful that it wasn't Covid, I had forgotten how miserable the flu can be. I quarantined in my bedroom for seventy-two hours. The first forty-eight hours I was so feverish and achy everywhere that I couldn't do anything but lie in bed anyway. The last twenty-four hours, I felt a little better, but I still had a fever and didn't want to expose my family. At that point, I started to feel very caged in. Although my Yorkie was good company, I missed my family. What's worse is that I missed trick-or-treating and fall festivals, which are things I love to watch my nine-year-old enjoy.

It's taken about three weeks to get back to my normal level of fatigue. I am typically disciplined with doing some form of exercise five to six days a week. This is one aspect of my health that is under my control, while so much is not, and I try to be consistent with it. Since I was unable to do anything for a few weeks, I really had to struggle to motivate myself to get back to it this week. I knew it would be hard. I knew I would be sore (and I was right).

I had to give myself a few lectures and then force myself, as the verse says, to "take a new grip with my tired hands" in order to "strengthen my weak knees." It probably goes without saying that I had to start very slow, with just a little walking and then some slow yoga stretches. The second part of Hebrews 12:12 really spoke to me, too, as lupus has affected my cerebellum and robbed me of good balance and coordination. I have to do frequent balance exercises in an attempt to prevent falls. I had to start these back, too, knowing I would not be very successful and trying not to get discouraged about that.

When I was working with clients, particularly stroke and TBI (traumatic brain injury) patients, I remember that sometimes the hardest part was their lack of self-motivation. Once I could figure out how to motivate someone to begin working, the rest of the treatment session was easier. Why is that initial motivation so hard? Is it our fear of failure? Is it the knowledge that it will be difficult? Is it the worry that it will take forever to get results? When a patient has a brain injury, sometimes there are changes or damage in the prefrontal cortex and/or limbic system that can negatively affect their ability to motivate themselves or even initiate an action. Although my brain certainly wasn't working well during my bout with the flu, I can't claim persistent brain damage, so why was it so hard for me to get back into my routine?

I struggled not only with exercise but also with doing my work/job on the computer as well as with daily chores. Everything was harder than I remembered. Here's what I discovered, though. If I could do a little bit more each day, then it gradually became easier. I teach online, so I started by reading a few forum posts rather than grading a paper or an exam. With chores, I could throw in a load of laundry, but I wasn't physically ready to vacuum the stairs.

When you're ill, work, exercise, and chores can all be difficult and, at times, even painful. If you look back at what Hebrews 12 discusses prior to this target verse, it's all about God's discipline and how we have to endure some things. We have to work hard, even when we don't want to. What might this "work" and "discipline" look like in our spiritual lives?

How about taking time out of your day to talk with a not-so-pleasant neighbor who seems a bit lonely? Maybe you could commit part of your Christmas money (set aside to buy family gifts) to a charity. How about sending an email to your child's teacher or your minister to show your appreciation? There are many things we could do that we are not doing because it would take a little discipline.

Whatever it is for you, I encourage you to "take a new grip with your tired hands" and get on with it. If you do one tiny thing today, you will be glad you got started in the right direction.

Heavenly Father, we need a little help with motivation today. If you could help us get started with something small, then we would not feel quite as overwhelmed with all our tasks. Please give us the motivation and the strength to get going. We love you. Amen.

70. Joyful Sunset/ Joyful Child

Shout for joy, you heavens; rejoice, you earth, burst into song, you mountains! For the LORD comforts his people and will have compassion on his afflicted ones. —Isaiah 49:13 (NLT)

My family was fortunate enough to have a couple of days on the beach during the holidays. When we got there after a long car trip, it was gorgeous sunset time, with vivid blue and orange colors among the waves. It could not have been more beautiful! I know you've seen a sunset, but have you seen a joyful sunset? A joyful sunset shows the earth and heavens rejoicing in a color song! After observing this from the condo balcony, we just had to get to the shore. Despite that it was the beginning of winter, we ran down to get our toes in the sand. Standing on the dark beach in sweats, jacket, and gloves—but bare feet—was exhilarating. I found that you can still have a great time at the beach, even when it's not warm.

My nine-year-old daughter was so thrilled to be there that she spontaneously began dancing and turning cartwheels in the sand. My husband and I laughed and hugged as we watched her. Such joy in the moment! Isn't this how we all should live, with the faith and joy of a child in the present?

Bogged down with illness, pain, emotions, finances, and work, we often forget to join in with the praise of the earth. Sometimes we need an earth-moment to remind us and to help us tolerate all the pain. We are then once again aware of the goodness, beauty, and compassion of the Lord.

As I write, we are preparing to welcome Jesus Christ at Christmas—the tiny, baby-shaped gift of hope, joy, and compassion. I want to attempt to be present in joy and praise. No matter what season you're in right now, despite your struggles, seek out the beauty of the stars, the snow, the birds, the sunset. Despite the pain, let the laughter and joy of the children around you wash into your soul. Rejoice and praise God! Breathe it all in, and then see if your burden might be just a little bit lighter.

Heavenly Father, thank you for the joyful sunsets and sunrises of the earth. Thank you also for the joyful actions of children, especially at Christmas. May the healing water of your beauty, compassion, and joy fill our hearts, our souls, and, yes, even our diseased bodies this season and every season. Amen.

71. Bye-Bye Sparkle

"Look! The virgin will conceive a child! She will give birth to a son, and they will call him Immanuel, which means 'God is with us.'" —Matthew 1:23 (NLT)

It's almost Christmas as I write this, and I'm sad for a rather silly reason. I even feel guilty for being sad. My nine-year-old announced this morning that she figured out that Sparkle (our Elf on the Shelf) isn't real, which led her to the thought that Santa isn't real. Her entire life, during the month of December, she has been in awe of Sparkle. She whispers to her, anticipates her coming, and can't wait to get up in the morning to see where Sparkle moved overnight. She never touched her because that would "break the magic" and she would fly back to the North Pole. This is the end of an era, although I knew it was coming when the Tooth Fairy "died" three months ago.

I'm sad because my children are growing up, and young children are fun, with all the extra Christmas magic. It certainly doesn't help that my other child is a senior in high school, but the issue of that grief is for another blog. My time as a mother of young children is ending, and that is sad for me. Maybe some of you can relate.

After picking up Sparkle and telling us she is just a doll, my young daughter proclaimed loudly, "But I *do* believe in Santa"—using air quotes—"so that I can get the extra gifts." Here's where my guilt comes in. This is certainly not what Christmas is about. In thinking this through, I'm coming around to the thought that no more Santa/ Elf can actually become a positive thing for our family. Christmas is about Christ and anticipating his coming—not the coming of a red and white doll or a large red and white man. My daughter accepted Christ and was baptized a year ago. As her young faith is growing, perhaps doing away with the magical distractions of North Pole events will give her more time to reflect on what is truly important in the Advent season.

Christmas still has lots of magic, of course. The story of baby Jesus, "God is with us," humbly born in a manger is magical. Our mysterious and captivating God loved us beyond all our ability to comprehend such love, and manifested this love by sending God's only Son to this flawed earth. God loved us so much that God wanted to be among us and with us in a very real way.

If you are struggling with nausea and pain today, know that God is with you. If you are wondering how to pay the bills, know that God is with you. If you are facing another chemo treatment, know that God is with you. If there is an empty chair at your table this year, know that God is with you. No one loves you more than God, and no one is with you and for you more than God. That is magical.

Lord God, thank you for the magical, yet very real, gift of your Son Jesus. Thank you for sending him to be with us, no matter what we face today. Help us to share with others a little of the love you bestow on us. Amen.

72. Extend Grace

Jesus, overhearing, shot back, "Who needs a doctor: the healthy or the sick? Go figure out what this Scripture means: 'I'm after mercy, not religion.' I'm here to invite outsiders, not coddle insiders." —Matthew 9:12-13 (NLT)

Do you concern yourself more with religious rituals or with extending mercy and grace to others?

Sometimes people get so bogged down with "religious" things that they miss the opportunity to be the light of Christ to others. I know because I've done this. At one time of my life, I was very concerned with being the chair of the education committee in my church and teaching a Bible/book study there, but I wasn't thinking enough about how I could serve the people outside my church. Church activities are good, but we are also called to work outside those walls.

I sometimes feel as though people with chronic illness can easily become part of the forgotten. Maybe they can't get to church often in the morning due to morning arthritis pain and stiffness. Maybe they can't attend a nighttime committee meeting because lupus causes them to be too fatigued at the end of the day. Maybe this is you.

However, maybe you/they *can* serve other "forgotten" people. It could be other people with chronic pain and chronic illnesses. It could also be someone older than you, who can no longer independently drive. If you can't get out to visit this person due to a risk to your health or your own debilitating illness, could you possibly reach out in another way?

If you are currently confined to your bed as a result of bone-crushing fatigue or severe pain, can you manage a brief FaceTime call or Zoom meeting? I've had many of these from my bed. There is no makeup or fancy wardrobe required! If you are not comfortable being seen right now (butterfly lupus rash? psoriasis?), then how about a brief phone call to let someone know that you're thinking of them?

Finally, if you're in too much pain for even a call, a simple text that states you said a prayer for *their* pain would be meaningful. However, don't forget to follow through and do this immediately (before your brain fog kicks in again). You don't have to drag someone inside a church building in order to serve them. We can all be there for each other in whatever limited capacity we are able to manage on that particular day.

For those of you blessed with health, please remember to extend grace to those who may appear "unreliable" when they frequently miss committee meetings or church services. You don't know what they are dealing with that day. Someone may wake up so stiff and sore in the morning that they can't manage to get dressed and go anywhere. Sometimes people are so fatigued at night that there's nothing left to give. We are called to extend mercy, grace, love, and encouragement freely, while forgetting the religious agenda.

Heavenly Father, help us to extend mercy and grace to others. Help us to reach out and serve those outside our church community, as well as the "forgotten" inside. Amen.

73. Lost Its Sheen

And now, dear children, remain in fellowship with Christ so that when he returns, you will be full of courage and not shrink back from him in shame. —1 John 2:28 (NLT)

As I write, we're at the beginning of a new year. But this bright, shiny new year has lost quite a bit of its sheen for me already, due to chronic pain and illness. This week, I have been struggling with chronic back pain as well as waking up with a migraine most days of the week and dealing with arthritis in my hand. What is much worse, however, is that my nine-year-old caught Covid the week she returned to school after the new year. We have had to isolate her in her room for a week now due to my high-risk autoimmune status. I feel guilty because it's my fault that we have to be so careful. I feel like an abusive parent forcing a young child to stay in her room and letting her out once a day for fresh air in the backyard, like a prison inmate.

My heart welled with tears yesterday when she said, "My own mother won't even touch me." That hurt. I know that this, too, shall pass, but it hurts *now*. My back hurts; my head hurts; my heart hurts. To sustain, I need courage.

There are those out there who are suffering so much more. Perhaps the chronic pain/disease is so bad right now that you are unable to get out of bed and care for your sick child. Perhaps your child is even in the hospital right now, and your heart is hurting more than mine has ever hurt.

I have no answers, but I have 1 John 2:28. I believe that we can draw courage by remaining in the fellowship of Christ. If you believe in God, spend time with God. If you don't or can't believe right now, then lean on someone who does. Let them hold you up and pray for you. Reach out for courage.

God can sustain you through this day of pain and disease, and God can sustain you through this pandemic or whatever else is happening in your world today. We are weary, but God can and will give us courage to endure.

Lord God, I am so tired of all this pain and sickness. Would you just make it stop? If not, can you please give me the courage to face it all again today? Can you give me a friend to lean on? Thank you for listening, as always. Amen.

74. Future Self

So we are always confident, even though we know that as long as we live in these bodies we are not at home with the Lord. For we live by believing and not by seeing. Yes, we are fully confident, and we would rather be away from these earthly bodies, for then we will be at home with the Lord. So whether we are here in this body or away from this body, our goal is to please him." —2 Corinthians 5:6-9 (NLT)

I'm mad at my body this week. Do you ever get mad at your body for not functioning the way it should? I'm particularly mad at my brain and nervous system, as I had four migraine days in a row. Today (so far) I'm okay and yesterday I was okay, but the four days prior to that were miserable. I've noticed that when I have consecutive days of feeling absolutely terrible, I begin to get really frustrated with my body. I try to feed it healthy food and exercise it and drink healthy water and take my nutritional supplements, and yet it betrays me. It's enough to make me want to give up all the healthy habits I've worked so hard to implement, since nothing seems to be working.

However, now that I don't have a migraine and am able to think clearly, I know that's not the right course. I need to do everything under my control to become and stay healthy, even if I don't always get the results (like little to no pain) that I want. I need to refrain from giving up because a certain day (or days) isn't going well. Instead, I need to look to the future and build myself up in preparation for something better.

Bible verses like 2 Corinthians 5:6-9 give me hope. I'm not attached to this deficient body. I'm ready to either trade it in or to take on a dramatically upgraded version in my future with Jesus.

Chronic illness patients often say they feel like a shadow of their former selves. Was there a time, like in your twenties, when you felt healthy and strong, but now you barely recognize that person in the mirror?

I was thinking about this as I reread portions of *Surprised by Hope* by N. T. Wright (2008) today. He writes,

> We sometimes speak of someone who's been very ill as being a shadow of their former self. If Paul is right, a Christian in the present life is a mere shadow of his or her future self, the self that person will be when the body that God has waiting in his heavenly storeroom is brought out, already made to measure, and put on over the present one—or over the self that will still exist after bodily death. (154)

That passage was very encouraging to me this morning, and I hope it brings a spark of hope to you. We are *all* shadows! It's okay if we are just a shadow of what we once were because, as believers, we have a future self coming that is so much stronger and healthier and more beautiful than we have ever dreamed of being. Isn't that wonderful news for all of us struggling with movement and weakness and pain?

What's more is that we have a purpose and a goal, which is to please the Lord, as the passage above states. We have work to do, even if we can't currently do it without pain and sickness. While we do this work, however we can manage it, we can believe not only in a pain-free future but also in a future of love and communion with Christ.

Lord, thank you for the reassurance of a future self, filled with your life and love. In the meantime, as we struggle with these painful bodies, please give us the strength to do the work of loving you and loving others. Amen.

75. Can't Do It Alone

"Talk to him, and put the words in his mouth. I will be with both of you as you speak, and I will instruct you both in what to do." —Exodus 4:15 (NLT)

Exodus 4:15 needs context. If you don't remember the story of Moses, read Exodus 3 and 4. God asked Moses to do a huge task. He was hesitant, thinking he couldn't do it. He actually argued with God and told him he didn't want to do it. At first, according to the Bible, the Lord was angry with Moses because he didn't trust God enough. After all, God wouldn't ask him to do something that was impossible. Quickly, though, God's anger and frustration turned to compassion. God realized Moses needed a companion to help him through this difficult task. God sent his brother to be by his side. This story reminds me of Adam needing Eve in the garden (Gen 2:18).

Sometimes—often—we need people to help us through. We think we're strong and can handle everything on our own, but we need to lean on others when it's difficult. God realizes that though God is with us, strengthening us, we may need a tangible human next to us. Sometimes we need to talk things out with a close friend. Sometimes we need to study things with a group of believers. Other times, we just need a hug or a hand to hold.

Being an introvert, I like a lot of alone time. Yet I realize my need for people, too. I need my family, my friends, my group of believers, and others who have chronic illness. When I am struggling, I need them more. When I am not struggling, I try to listen to see if they need an extra nudge of support from me.

In life, this give-and-take can break down. It happens a lot in chronic illness, according to research. People who are chronically ill don't want to need people a lot. They hate it that they need help, but they do. It becomes even harder when their designated "people" don't want to provide that help over and over. Maybe they are supportive initially, but they soon realize they can't give as much. They resent having to repeatedly set aside their own goals to help their partner. Some are simply selfish and see their partner as an inconvenience that's not going away. Others have too much of their own stuff to deal with and are incapable of this kind of love.

I was diagnosed with lupus one February. My ex-husband told me that he wanted out in March. He survived only one month, knowing his wife would always be sick. That "for-better-or-for-worse" thing wasn't true for him. Unfortunately, I'm not alone in that story. My rheumatologist (and statistics) said this is an extremely common occurrence and one he deals with weekly with his patients. I've watched this happen to friends with lupus, as their partners either can't take it or choose not to deal with it.

Here's the hope. My story didn't end there. My family, friends, and church were there when my partner was not. They were able to provide the kind of caregiving love and support I needed. Four years later, I found a new partner, one who was and is able to stick it out, no matter the day's symptoms.

If a partner or friend drifts away because you're ill and "not so fun" anymore, it can seem like you now have to deal with chronic illness and chronic loneliness, which is an unbearable burden. If you're in that place right now, I don't believe that's the end of your story. I want you to reach out and look around you. Can you find a friend or a neighbor or a church member or a counselor who will listen? I believe God will provide a human to sit with you in your pain. It's not that the Lord isn't enough, but God built us to need community. God knows you need this and will provide it.

If you have no one, pray that God will provide someone. You have a part to play, though. You must not shut yourself inside your house and retreat into your pain. Ask God for the strength to meet a friend for coffee or to speak to a neighbor who is outside. Attend a support group meeting or go to a church. Contact someone, even if it is only online. You have to take a first step, but I promise that it will be worth it.

Heavenly Father, please provide someone for everyone. Let those who are suffering know that they are not truly alone. When they are abandoned by someone who can't handle their illness, lift them up with a smile or embrace from a loving person. You are so, so good, but they need to see that good in other people, too. Thank you for never abandoning us in our pain. Amen.

76. Wasting Time

Even if we feel guilty, God is greater than our feelings, and he knows everything. —1 John 3:20 (NLT)

For God is greater than our worried hearts and knows more about us than we do ourselves. —1 John 3:20 (MSG)

I was having extensive Mom-guilt last week about something long in the past when a wise friend shared 1 John 3:20 with me and told me to quit wasting time feeling guilty. It was good advice. Maybe you need to hear it, too. The more I thought about it, the more this Maya Angelou quote (Smith 2021) floated into my mind: "I did then what I knew how to do. Now that I know better, I do better."

I concluded that I did the best I could at the time with my parenting decisions. Hopefully, I learn each year and get a little better at it. I'm guessing all parents want a do-over about something (or several somethings) in the past, but they were probably doing the best they could at the time. Come to think of it, my parents weren't perfect, either, although they seem pretty close!

Guilt and worry over past decisions, however, is definitely not limited to parenting. You may feel guilty over something you did or said in a past friendship or a previous marriage. You can even feel guilty about your health. I think those of us with chronic illness go down that path fairly frequently.

I was just talking with a friend yesterday who was wondering what she did to cause her chronic illness. Although this line of thinking gets you nowhere, I understood the process. I've done this repeatedly. A chronic illness makes you question all of your past decisions, thinking if you had made a different choice, then you might not be sick. I have beaten myself up for eating lots of fast food in college, for example. What if it contributed to my lupus diagnosis in my thirties? Why didn't I choose to eat salads every day in that college cafeteria? Perhaps some of your choices have contributed to your illness. Maybe none of them did. Either way, it's in the past, and you're wasting time feeling guilty or worrying about it.

Instead of wasting time in the past, let's think about today. How can you take care of yourself today? How can you be a good parent or friend today? Here's what I'm going to do. I'm going to eat a healthy dinner tonight and commit to exercising tomorrow. I'm going to stop typing this devotion and go join my daughter for a movie night (as she requested five minutes ago). Plan for good decisions now, and stop wasting time on the past.

Dear God, why do I waste so much time in the past when you have given me a beautiful present? Help me to make wise choices for today and stop worrying about things that are behind me. Amen.

77. A Record of Pain

You've kept track of my every toss and turn through the sleepless nights, each tear entered in your ledger, each ache written in your book. —Psalm 56:8 (MSG)

You keep track of all my sorrows. You have collected all my tears in your bottle. You have recorded each one in your book. —Psalm 56:8 (NLT)

I have been trying to help someone I know who also has lupus. She hasn't been dealing with this disease long, but it is progressing fast. She feels like her life is over. She can't think (brain fog) and had to quit her job. Her marriage is falling apart since her husband doesn't seem to be able to deal with her "changes." She can't sleep because of the relentless pain. She has an advanced degree she can't use, and she can't pay her student loans. She lives in a fog of pain and confusion day after day. I can relate to so much of her story.

She may feel that she is alone, but she is not. I firmly believe that God is weeping with her. As Psalm 56:8 says, God keeps track of each tear she cries and records every pain in her body. I don't understand why she has to suffer like this, but I know that it does not go unnoticed by our Savior. Not only does God love her deeply and hurt with her daily, but somehow, someway God will use this pain for good.

I'm at a relatively calm place with my lupus currently, but I know what it's like to be in the dark middle of it. A painful, swollen, rash-covered, confused body has a hard time finding daily hope. Sometimes someone living in the worst of it needs another person who has been there but found their way forward. They need to know that someone understands what they are going through and will listen to them wail and whine through it. They need someone to give them hope when they can't find it themselves.

I hope I'm that someone sometimes. I hope that you are encouraged by God through me. I hope that God can use my past dark times of suffering to help you through yours. When I was in a severe lupus flare for several years, thinking my life was over, the only other person I knew with lupus (who had mild symptoms at the time) took me to a support group. Almost twenty years later, that woman now has severe symptoms, while mine are milder. My point is that we need each other, and we need to allow God's love, hope, and encouragement to flow through us to others, particularly in our "better times."

You may feel like you are suffering alone, but countless people have been there and are there now. Even if no one physically holds your hand through your suffering, you can rest in the fact that God is collecting all your tears. God sees you. God sees how you suffer each day. Your pain does not go unnoticed.

It may not always seem like it, but there are also people out there who care. There are others with chronic pain. There are caring doctors, nurses, physical therapists, and chiropractors who will do their best to ease your pain. There are support groups, which can easily turn into friendships. If you haven't found them, please keep looking.

As I told my new friend the other day, it may not seem like it, but I believe that you will get better. I believe that your life is not over and that you have a purpose. It's okay if you can't believe it today because I believe it for you, and I will try to help you find your hope.

Lord God, suffering is so hard day after day. Be with my friends whose lives are currently filled with pain. May they believe the truth that you notice every ache and collect every tear. May they also find more friends who can relate and help carry them through this. Please give them strength, hope, and healing. Amen.

78. There's No Fish

Don't blame us for the sins of our parents. Hurry up and help us; we're at the end of our rope. You're famous for helping; God, give us a break." —Psalm 79:8 (MSG)

My young daughter has a betta fish she got for her ninth birthday. Who knew it would still be living ten months later? Anyway, we had an additional fish that cleaned the tank. It recently vanished (bad betta!), so we went to the fish store last week to get another one. As we were driving away from the store, I heard a cry in the backseat: "There's no fish!" Sure enough, when I pulled back into the parking spot to check, I realized I had just purchased a bag of water! The salesperson at the fish store was extremely embarrassed and immediately harassed by his coworkers for that mistake.

As I write this, we are in the third year of a depressing, draining pandemic. In addition, Russia invaded Ukraine last week and is threatening the use of nuclear weapons. My heart breaks at the suffering of the Ukrainian people I see on TV. My children are asking if we're about to have World War III. I want to reassure them that is not a possibility, but I can't. I never meant to raise children in such times. Through the emotional stress of it all, some of us physically feel awful, as we are also dealing with chronic illness: autoimmune disease, heart disease, long Covid, etc. It can feel like you've got nothing good, no pretty fish, just an empty bag of water. It feels like "we're at the end of our rope," or as the NLT says, "on the brink of despair."

It's okay to cry out to God, saying, "Give us a break!" I think we are instructed to cry out. Tell God everything that you are feeling and everything you are dealing with. Scream and cry if it helps. If you are struggling, don't go to church or out in society or on FaceTime with a friend and pretend you're fine with life as it is. Be real and honest with both God and others. This is a difficult time. Americans are in no way suffering like the Ukrainians, but life is hard for nearly everyone right now.

Remember, though, that as you're asking God to give you a break (from stress, from nausea, from pain, from fever), you are called to give others a break, too. Maybe your friend is a little grumpy or not as fun as usual. Maybe your child is acting out, feeling stressed by the pandemic and war they don't understand. Have compassion on them, just as God does for you. Support each other, and cry out in prayer together. Never, ever forget that God loves you and is with you, even in this . . . especially in this.

Dear God, we are in despair with our health and we are in despair with the state of the world. We are frightened and at the end of our ropes. Hear us as we cry. Sustain us. Have compassion on us and enable us to have compassion on and patience with our neighbors. Amen.

79. Use Those Flatland Times

God remembered us when we were down, His love never quits. Rescued us from the trampling boot, His love never quits. Takes care of everyone in time of need. His love never quits. Thank God, who did it all! His love never quits!
—Psalm 136:23-26 (MSG)

I know three women who are struggling to get out of bed, can't work, and can't think straight right now due to the devastating disease of lupus. They are angry at what life has dealt them. I get it—I've been them. I want it to be over for them, this daily struggle. I want them to be well and to return to their lives. And yet I can't make the disease process stop tearing apart their bodies from the inside. I can't make them stop worrying about their finances, their families, and their health. What I can do is encourage them and reassure them that God's love and care is still present for them, even when they can't feel it.

I also know four women whose husbands were all recently diagnosed with cancer. The stress on their faces is visible as they struggle to support and take care of their newly fragile husbands, while also trying to keep their children from breaking apart emotionally. One woman's teenager is suddenly afraid to drive anywhere. Another woman's child now can't sleep through the night. In addition to worrying about their husbands' suffering, these women are worried about the consequences on their children and their finances. They are trying to hold life together amid the unpredictability of the future. In Psalm 136, we are promised that God will take care of us in our time of need and will love us through it. Maybe it's partly my job to remind my friends of this.

You know people who are struggling as well. Those of us who have a relatively good life right now know that our time of trial is coming. Life seems to be a winding road of dips and hills, with some boring flat roads along the way with not much going on. The longer I live, the more I appreciate those flatland times, those routine days. If you are currently in a season of monotonous flatland, give thanks to God that you aren't in a valley right now. Use your extra energy during this time to reach out to someone who is struggling, and share God's promise of love and care.

If you are the one stuck at the bottom of a canyon right now, struggling with sickness and/or grief like my friends, please read and meditate on Psalm 136:23-26. Believe and know deep in your soul that God has not and will never abandon you to suffer in this alone. God's love *never* quits.

Almighty God, I thank you that I am in a season of relative stability right now. Please help me to use the blessing of this flatland time to strengthen and encourage others who are struggling to survive the day. Please make your presence and your loving care obvious to them through friends and family. Amen.

80. No, Me Do It!

Spread for me a banquet of praise, serve High God a feast of kept promises, and call for help when you're in trouble—I'll help you, and you'll honor me. —Psalm 50:15 (MSG)

I'm not great at asking for help. My husband is always saying, "Why didn't you ask me to carry that?" My migraine has to be at a pain level of 9 or 10 before I'll admit that I can't make dinner or run an errand. I won't ask for help until I absolutely *have* to ask for help.

As an example, two years ago, I suddenly had severe pain while in the grocery store with my kids. This pain felt like nothing I had ever felt. It was beyond a 10. Looking back, I shouldn't have driven my family home. I should have had the cashier call an ambulance. It turned out, when I finally went to the hospital, that I had an ovarian torsion (a twisted ovary) and needed emergency surgery.

Is it human nature to insist on doing things ourselves? How many times have you heard a toddler emphatically announce, "No, me do it"? We want to take care of things on our own, even when it's not best for us.

Sometimes I even hate to ask God for help in prayer. Am I the only one? I often think that there are so many other people with more severe issues, so I pause. Last week, though, I read Psalm 50:15: "call for help when you're in trouble—I'll help you, and you'll honor me." God is telling us to ask for help. God *will* help us, and through the process of asking, we will honor God.

I'm not completely sure how asking for help honors God. Is it because we must humble ourselves and admit our dependence? Is it because we acknowledge our need for God? Could it be a form of praise as we affirm our belief in a God who can do anything and everything?

Whatever the reason, God wants us to ask for help and wants to help us. God cares about *your* pain, *your* sleepless night, *your* fear, and *your* sickness. So no more hesitating—for either of us. When you're dealing with chronic pain and illness, you are going to need some help to make it. There will be days when you need a lot of help—from family and friends and from God.

God, I hate to ask for help, yet it's necessary when I am sick. How do I get over this? Help me to acknowledge that I can't do everything. Thank you for the reassurance through your word that you want us to ask for help. Thank you for loving me and caring about my pain. Amen.

81. Waiting, Risking, Hoping

I've kept my feet on the ground, I've cultivated a quiet heart. Like a baby content in its mother's arms, my soul is a baby content. Wait, Israel, for God. Wait with hope. Hope now; hope always!" —Psalm 131:2-3 (MSG)

My youngest daughter was supposed to have surgery this week, and we have all been worried about it for nearly two months. The afternoon before the surgery, after we had already paid our bill in full and taken off work, the surgeon's office called to cancel. They still have not rescheduled but said it would be two more months before they could do it.

When told after school, my daughter cried for an hour. She kept saying that she just wanted to get it over with and stop worrying about it all the time. As her mother, I wanted the same, but instead we have to wait longer. It's so hard to wait, particularly when you're waiting for something painful. It's hard to wait with hope.

People with chronic illness do a lot of waiting, like waiting in doctors' offices and waiting for test results and waiting to see if a new medication will make us any better. When you feel awful every day, it can be easy to slip into despair and depression, to tire of waiting for life to improve. To fight this, we must cultivate hope through our faith in Christ.

I recently read *The Book of Joy*. In this book, the late Bishop Desmond Tutu is quoted as saying,

Despair can come from deep grief, but it can also be a defense against the risks of bitter disappointment and shattering heart-break. Resignation and cynicism are easier, more self-soothing postures that do not require the raw vulnerability and tragic risk of hope. To choose hope is to step firmly forward into the howling wind, baring one's chest to the elements, knowing that, in time, the storm will pass. (122)

The book goes on to say that hope is the antidote to despair but that hope requires faith.

I have observed chronically ill patients give in to despair, resigned to be sick and miserable for the rest of their lives. By self-fulfilling prophecy, they then become depressed people with unhappy lives. Instead, we must find the courage through our faith to step forward each day to seek good. While we are sick, we wait with hope for healing, but we also actively look for the good things in our current lives, cultivating gratitude. People who live this way may still be in physical pain, yet their lives are not completely miserable. They are able to find moments of joy.

Heavenly Father, it often seems that the storm of illness will never pass, but we know that one day we will no longer suffer pain. Thank you for this promise. For now, please give us the courage to face the day with hope and the gratitude to recognize the good things in our lives. Amen.

Works Cited

Chambers, Oswald. 2017 (revised). *My Utmost for His Highest.* Grand Rapids, MI: Our Daily Bread Publishing.

Chapman, Stephen Curtis. 1996. "Let Us Pray." *Songs of Life.*

"Christian Contemplation." Updated June 2017. *Wikipedia.* https:// en.wikipedia.org/wiki/Christian_contemplation.

Dalai Lama, Desmond Tutu, and Douglas Abrams. 2016. *The Book of Joy: Lasting Happiness in a Changing World.* London, GB: Cornerstone Publishers.

Eldredge, John. 2011. *Beautiful Outlaw.* New York: Hachette Book Group.

Holy Bible: English Standard Version. 2016. Wheaton, IL: Crossway.

Holy Bible: New Living Translation. 2020. Carol Stream, IL. Tyndale House Publishers.

Llewelyn, Robert. 1985. *All Shall be Well: The Spirituality of Julian of Norwich for Today.* Mahwah, NJ: Paulist Press.

Peterson, Eugene. 2002. *The Message: The Bible in Contemporary Language.* Colorado Springs: NavPress.

Smith, David. 2022. *100 Inspirational Quotes by Maya Angelou: A Boost of Wisdom and Inspiration from the Legendary Poet.* Independently published.

Smith, Michael W. 2018. "Surrounded." *Surrounded.*

Wright, N. T. 2008. *Surprised by Hope: Rethinking Heaven, the Resurrection, and the Mission of the Church.* San Francisco: HarperOne.

www.ingramcontent.com/pod-product-compliance
Lightning Source LLC
Chambersburg PA
CBHW062103080426
42734CB00012B/2731